The word "sin" is no longer spoken, nessing firsthand the fruits thereof. Allen Webster not only resurrects the Biblical truth about sin, but he also delivers a perfect prescription for how to navigate the tough waters that many young adults face today. In his latest book *All the Devil's Apples Have Worms*, Webster confronts timely topics in a straightforward manner, sharing Biblical wisdom in a way that few can. While some individuals are content to simply "monitor" the spiritual sickness of our culture, Allen Webster takes his finger off the pulse and uses that finger to help direct our culture back in line with God's Word. Many thanks for the time and study put into this great tool. I pray that this excellent classroom book will reveal Satan's spoiled fruit and will help build a generation of warriors for God.

—BRAD HARRUB
Editor, *Think* Magazine

More than ever, teens in the 21st century are in need of the right kind of guidance. Packed full of Scripture, common sense, and sound advice, this book brings to light (with great specificity) the destructiveness of sin and the blessings of obedience. Parents, preachers, elders and youth ministers need to get this book into the hands of their teens. Better yet, spend a quarter studying it with them.

—ERIC LYONS
Author, *The Anvil Rings* Vol. 1 and Vol. 2

Wow! *The Devil's Apples* is a fresh take on some of the oldest sins that still stain the personal integrity of too many Christians. Standing firmly in the middle of the Book, Webster presents a balanced but conservative view of what it means to practice true righteousness from the inside out. Our young people need more Christian leaders to speak so plainly on how we should live as Christians. For that matter, we all need to be reminded of the radical, life-changing roots of true discipleship.

—MATT VEGA
Associate Professor of Law
Faulkner University

ALL OF THE DEVIL'S APPLES HAVE WORMS

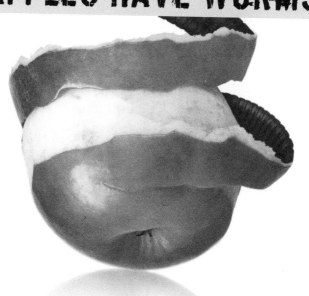

ALLEN WEBSTER

(c) 2010 Heart to Heart Publishing Inc. Printed and bound in the United States of America. All rights reserved. No part of this book may be reproduced or transmitted in any form or by any means, electronic or mechanical, including photocopying, recording, or by an information storage and retrieval system-except by a reviewer who may quote brief passages in a review to be printed in a magazine, newspaper, or on the Web-without permission in writing from the publisher. For information please contact Heart to Heart Publishing Inc., PO Box 520, Jacksonville, AL 36265.

Although the author and publisher have made every effort to ensure the accuracy and completeness of information contained in this book, we assume no responsibility for errors, inaccuracies, omissions, or any inconsistency herein.
Any slights of people, places, or organizations are unintentional.

First Printing 2010

ISBN 978-1-60644-075-9

ATTENTION CHURCHES, UNIVERSITIES, COLLEGES, AND ORGANIZATIONS: Quantity discounts are available on bulk purchases of this book for educational and gift purposes, or as premiums for increasing magazine subscriptions or renewals. Special books or book excerpts can also be created to suit specific needs. For more information, please contact Heart to Heart Publishing Inc., PO Box 520, Jacksonville, AL 36265. Phone: 877-338-3397.

Web site: www.housetohouse.com

❖ ❖ ❖

To my parents
Milton and Diana Webster
who taught me the principles
found in this book
from my youth (2 Timothy 3:15).

TABLE OF CONTENTS

Note: If you are teaching on a 13-week quarter system, omit chapters 6, 11, and 15 (but encourage students to read them for homework).

Chapter 1: ***A Bad Word in the Bible*** 7

Chapter 2: ***Birds of a Feather*** 19

Chapter 3: ***Watch Out for Bad Apples*** 25

Chapter 4: ***Don't Trip Over Your Tongue on the Way to Heaven*** 31

Chapter 5: ***Give Your Tobacco to a Billy Goat*** 43

Chapter 6: ***The Pros and Cons of Starting the Smoking Habit*** 53

Chapter 7: ***Hollywood or Holy God? (A Christian TV Guide)*** 63

Chapter 8: ***Dealing with Sexual Temptation*** 73

Chapter 9: ***Should Christian Teens Dance?*** 85

Chapter 10: ***What about Swimming?*** 95

Chapter 11: ***How to Protect Yourself from Date Rape*** 107

Chapter 12: ***Don't Drink and Date*** 117

Chapter 13: ***Wait Till the Honeymoon?*** 125

Chapter 14: ***Pornography's Pain*** 133

Chapter 15: ***Odd Odds to Bet On*** 139

Chapter 16: ***Launch Out with Jesus*** 147

CHAPTER 1

A BAD WORD IN THE BIBLE

There are certain places people expect to find "bad words." They are written in truck stop bathrooms and construction sites. Sailors have a reputation for knowing quite a few bad words. Locker rooms after a tough loss may echo with some unprintable jargon. There is no shortage of them in R-rated movies and in most war novels. But who would never expect to find a "bad word" in the Bible? Curse words are often called "four-letter words" but the Bible's bad word only has three letters. This word is the fountain of woe and the mother of sorrows. It is as universal as humanity. This word has caused all the war, violence, hatred, sorrow, and pain in the world. This word nailed the Son of God to the Cross. Every tear you have ever shed, every pain you have had to endure, every sorrow that has clouded you day, every casket of a loved one you have lowered into the ground has, either directly or indirectly been because of this word. It is the ruin of life.

The word is *sin*.

J. W. McGarvey once said, "I would esteem above every other gift that could be bestowed upon me as a preacher the power to adequately conceive what sin is and to adequately set it before the people." The Bible uses its "bad word" a lot—547 times.

The first time is in Genesis 4:7 when Moses wrote, "Sin lieth at the door." Ever since, sin has been crouching at humanity's door. This was not the first appearance of sin, but it was the first mention of sin, and the first appearance of the final fruit of sin. Remember James wrote, "when lust hath conceived, it bringeth forth sin: and sin, when it is finished, bringeth forth death" (James 1:15). Lust had conceived the first murder, the first death of man, as the finished work of sin. Genesis begins the long, sad chapter of sin, a chapter that comes to a close only with the last chapter of the Bible, when there shall be no more curse (Revelation 22:3). It is interesting, by the way, that the word *sin* is not found in this book about heaven (Revelation).

Let's look at three Bible figures for sin.

SIN AS POISONOUS FRUIT

We do not know what kind of fruit the devil offered Eve in Eden. Perhaps it was a peach or a plum or a pomegranate. It could have been a mango or a fig. She might have tasted a pear or a grapefruit. The *los freseros* strawberry pickers of California seem to think it was a strawberry (although they don't grow on trees). They call strawberries *la fruta del diablo* which means "the fruit of the devil." (It could be because they spend ten hours a day in the hot sun, bent at the waist, picking those little red berries we enjoy from the supermarket.)

Or Eve could have seen a Red Delicious apple, recognizing that it was "good for food, and that it was pleasant to the eyes, and a tree to be desired to make one wise." She ate the fruit "and gave also unto her husband with her; and he did eat" (Genesis 3:6).

Whatever it was, it was defective. That "apple" had a worm in it. Satan promised her freedom, but Eve found slavery. He implied that she would be like God, but she could not even stand any more in His presence. She thought her life would improve, but afterward she spent her time hiding in the bushes. Life went downhill fast after that first bite of sin.

Today the devil has lots of choices in his fruit stand, but every last piece has a worm. Every bite is spiritual poison.

It is interesting that the first sin involved fruit. Fruit is one of the most widely found ideas in the Bible. It is used in both positive and negative senses. Jesus taught, "For every tree is known by his own fruit" (Luke 6:44). The blessed man of Psalm 1 is famously compared to "a tree planted by the rivers of water, that bringeth forth his fruit in his season" (1:3). Children are referred to as the "fruit of the womb" (Psalm 127:3). Jesus is the vine that brings forth much fruit (John 15:5). The Lord's supper has the "fruit of the vine" (Luke 22:18). We are urged to possess the "fruit of the Spirit" (Galatians 5:22–23). The last chapter of the Bible says that heaven will have fruit. In fact "the tree of life" is identified as having twelve different kinds of fruit—which it bears for one month at a time (Revelation 22:2).

Fruit can also refer to sin (Psalm 21:10). Solomon warned his son of the "bad apples" whose fruit the Lord would eventually pluck:

> Then shall they call upon me, but I will not answer; they shall seek me early, but they shall not find me: for that they hated knowledge, and did not choose the fear of the Lord: they would none of my counsel: they despised all my reproof. Therefore shall they eat of the fruit of their own way, and be filled with their own devices (Proverbs 1:28–31).

In the same vein, let's compare sin to wormy fruit, which is poisonous to the soul.

Sin poisons the mind. I don't know if worms are poisonous or not. It is unlikely that you would die from eating one, but you would definitely feel sick. On the other hand, there is no doubt that sin is poisonous. "The soul that sinneth, it shall die" (Ezekiel 18:20). "The wages of sin is death" (Romans 6:23). In the end sin "bringeth forth death" (James 1:15). All unforgiven sinners will experience the second death (Revelation 21:8).

ABC Evening News reported on an unusual work of modern art—a shotgun affixed to a chair. The art is to be viewed by sitting in the chair and looking directly down the gun barrel. The gun is loaded and set on a timer to fire at an undetermined moment within the next hundred years. The amazing thing is that people wait in line to sit and stare down that barrel! They all know the gun could go off at point-blank range at any moment, but they gamble that the fatal blast won't happen during their minute in the chair. Yes, it was foolhardy, yet many people who would not dream of sitting in that chair live a lifetime gambling that they can get away with sin. They eat poison fruit and think they'll never get sick. Foolishly they ignore the risk until the inevitable self-destruction.

Sin sickens. If you took a bite of an apple only to look down to find *half* a worm left in the apple, you'd feel sick. Sin sickens those who stop to reflect on their actions. Sin cost Samson his self-respect (Judges 16:25). How did that prodigal son feel about himself when he smelled of pigs? (Luke 15:14–16).

Our sins may never land us in a pigpen, but they do put us into disgrace. We don't feel good about ourselves when we have been eating forbidden fruit. Those who have abortions, for instance, often have long periods of depression. Criminals and prostitutes can come to loathe themselves. "Regular" sinners have trouble with guilt too. Young people who cheat on tests, tell lies, and mistreat others don't think well of themselves when the lights go out and the head hits the pillow.

Many who commit sexual sin go home and take a long shower to try to feel clean (but it does not work). College students call a girl's early morning trip from a boy's apartment to her dorm the "walk of shame." They might act as if sex is casual, but it is hard to ignore the loss of self-respect it engenders. Drug users try to hide their habit from others. Those who get drunk are often ashamed of their embarrassing or criminal behavior. Many young people have trouble looking at themselves in the mirror because they are sick of who they have become. You see, if you eat the devil's apple, you'll be sick.

Thankfully, God has the medicine that cures a sin-sick soul. He can remove the smell of the hogs and the bitter taste of sin. The blood of His Son is a cure-all for sin and guilt. Paul promises, "There is therefore now no condemnation to them which are in Christ Jesus, who walk not after the flesh, but after the Spirit" (Romans 8:1). Have you quit eating wormy apples and "tasted the good word of God"? (Hebrews 6:5). If not, "O taste and see that the Lord is good" (Psalm 34:8).

Sin disgusts others. If others saw you take that bite of half apple, half worm, everyone there would be disgusted. Your popularity would plummet. Sin also disgusts right thinking people. It divides and renders a person lonely. When Adam and Eve ate the forbidden fruit, one of the first results was a feeling of loneliness and separation from God. Samson must have felt isolated in that Gaza prison. Sin will certainly divide a teen from his God (Isaiah 59:1–2) and his divine purpose (Galatians 5:17–23; Romans 7:18–25), but it may also divide him from his family (Genesis 19) and from his spiritual brothers and sisters (2 Thessalonians 3:6). The ungodly will not be able to hold up their heads in the judgment (Psalm 1:5).

PART 2: SIN AS A THIEF

At some point in our lives, statistics tell us that most of us will be the victims of a thief (169.7 of every 1,000 people in any given year). Perhaps your car, house, or person has already been violated by the hands of an uninvited visitor. Regardless, we can say with confidence that there is one thief who has made mockery of every mature person. His name is Sin.

Sin steals the innocence from one's mind. Adam and Eve were as innocent as babies and as pure as honey in the comb *until* . . . the thief stole their innocence as the wind steals the smoke (Genesis 3). Their unparalleled purity became as irreplaceable as a broken egg. They hid from the God who had been their favorite companion. Their guilt drove them from their God and their God drove them from their paradise. The age of innocence was finished.

Though under different circumstances, and to varying degrees, we have all been robbed of our innocence by the same thief. Our purity lasts . . . *until* the thief of sin has made his entrance through the broken window of the mind and taken the irretrievable treasure known as innocence. *Until* our lips have tasted the bitterness of alcohol, *until* our lungs have breathed nicotine's smoke, *until* our vessels have coursed with gambler's adrenaline, *until* our eyes have feasted on the indecent, *until* our fingers have handled dishonest gain, *until* our feet have known the sand of forbidden paths, *until* our bodies have slept in fornication's bed, *until* our tongues have known the curl of the curse word, *until* our hands have clenched into anger's fist, *until* our knees have bowed in prayer to the wrong god. *Until.* Then it can never again be said (or thought), "I don't know what that sin is like."

For further study on these points, consult these verses:

- **alcohol**, Genesis 9:21-24; Proverbs 20:1; 23:29-33; Ephesians 5:18;
- **smoking**, 1 Corinthians 3:16-17; 6:19-20; 1 Peter 2:11;
- **gambling and dishonesty**, Matthew 7:12; 22:39; Romans 12:17; 13:9-10; Philippians 4:8; 2 Thessalonians 3:10;
- **pornography**, Matthew 5:8, 27-30; Romans 1:26-32; 6:12-14; Philippians 4:8; 1 Corinthians 6:18; 1 Thessalonians 5:22;
- **forbidden paths**, Proverbs 1:15; 2:9; 4:14, 18, 26; 5:6;
- **fornication**, Genesis 39; Proverbs 6:23-34; 1 Corinthians 6:9-20; Galatians 5:16, 19-21; 1 Thessalonians 4:1-6; 2 Timothy 2:22; Titus 2:12; Hebrews 13:4;
- **cursing**, Ephesians 4:29; James 3:10;
- **anger**, Ephesians 4:31; Colossians 3:8, 21;
- **wrong god**, 2 Kings 19:18; 2 Chronicles 13:9; Isaiah 37:19; Jeremiah 2:11; 5:7; 16:20.

Sin steals the comfort from one's pillow. Jacob pillowed his head on a stone, and found rest (Genesis 28:18), but the robbed man can rest his on a goose-down feather pillow and find none (Proverbs 13:15; cf. Ecclesiastes 2:23; Romans 3:16-18). "There is no peace, saith the LORD, unto the wicked" (Isaiah 48:22). She lies on her bed wishing she could undo the past but knowing that the clock of life can never be reversed. He closes his eyes to try to change the subject, but the mind flutters and returns to the same rotting carcass of sin's memory. She finally drifts into fitful sleep only to waken with the first thought of the sin that is ever before her, wishing it were a dream but knowing it is all too real. "The wicked man travaileth with pain all his days, and the number of years is hidden to the oppressor . . . Trouble and anguish shall make him afraid; they shall prevail against him, as a king ready to the battle" (Job 15:20, 24). Rest comes hard to a conscience pricked with a thousand needles of guilt. What an "evil thing and bitter" sin is (Jeremiah 2:19)!

Sin steals the self-confidence from a one's eye. The eye tells much about what a man thinks of himself. Jesus said, "The light of the body is the eye" (Matthew 6:22). As sins weigh on one's soul, it sometimes shows in his visual contact. Where once was a Christian confident in his power to wage war with Satan now stands a sinner feeling like a prisoner of war.

Where once stood a gymnast who had never fallen now falters a girl who doubts her gracefulness. Where once stood the proud boxer whose knees had never buckled now stands a man who hopes he can protect his chin. He is vulnerable, uncertain, and afraid the past may repeat itself. Job had his confidence stolen during his suffering. He said, "If I justify myself, mine own mouth shall condemn me: if I say, I am perfect, it shall also prove me perverse" (Job 9:20). Jesus, though He looked not at them, found some who could not face Him because of the condemnation of their consciences: "And they which heard it, being convicted by their own conscience, went out one by one, beginning at the eldest, even unto the last: and Jesus was left alone, and the woman standing in the midst" (John 8:9; cf. Romans 2:1).

Sin steals the influence from one's life. The Christian worker who once owned the respect of his peers now feels like a hypocrite among associates (cf. Romans 2:21-24). The trusted friend whose advice was once respected now finds that no one seeks his opinion. The father whose sons once longed to walk in his steps finds that they have other heroes. The husband who once enjoyed the unreserved devotion of his wife now finds he is the recipient of suspicious questions and reluctant trust. David's counselor, Ahithophel, joined Absalom's conspiracy against his familiar friend. He advised pursuit of David to finish him while he was weak, but Absalom spurned the traitor's wisdom and accepted Hushai's. "And when Ahithophel saw that his counsel was not followed, he saddled his donkey, and arose, and gat him home to his house, to his city, and put his household in order, and hanged himself, and died, and was buried in the sepulchre of his father" (2 Samuel 17:23). Sin had stolen his influence, so he felt that life was not worth living. How tragic!

Influence is one of a Christian's most valuable treasures. It is to be guarded even at great cost. Nehemiah said in the long ago: "Ought ye not to walk in the fear of our God because of the reproach of the heathen our enemies?" (5:9). The Christian's light must never lose its sparkle; her salt must never lose its flavor (Matthew 5:13-16); his leaven must never lose its contagion (Matthew 13:33). He must use "sound speech, that cannot be condemned; that he that is of the contrary part may be ashamed, having no evil thing to say" (Titus 2:8). She should "give none occasion to the adversary to speak reproachfully" (1 Timothy 5:14). He should have his "conversation honest among the Gentiles: that, whereas they speak against you as evildoers, they may by your good works, which they shall behold, glorify God in the day of visitation" (1 Peter 2:12; cf. 2:15; 3:16). Let vigilance keep her constant watch lest sin steal our power to lead others to Christ.

PART 3: SIN AS A PREDATOR (PROVERBS 13:21).

Temptation is pictured many ways in Scripture. James described temptation as the bait on a hook or in a trap (James 1:14), and as a womb pregnant with evil (James 1:15; cf. Psalm 7:14; Isaiah 59:4, 16). In Nathan's story, temptation was a friendly traveler who dropped in for a visit (2 Samuel 12:1-5). But to Cain, temptation was like a hungry beast lurking outside (Genesis 4:7), to which God warned him not to open the door (but he did anyway). In this section, let's focus on sin as a vicious animal.

Sin carefully stalks the sinner. Sin lies in wait for a sinner. "Sin lieth at the door" (Genesis 4:7) literally means, "Sin crouches, ready to attack." The idea is that additional sins were ready to join the anger and hatred already in Cain's heart. "Now that anger is in your heart, murder is at the door." Those who do not keep one of God's commands are in danger of committing more and more sins. The way of sin is downhill, and sinners go from bad to worse

(Numbers 32:14; Isaiah 1:5; 5:18; 30:1; Hosea 13:2; Romans 2:5; 2 Timothy 3:13).

When Jonah started away from God, he went "down" to Joppa (Jonah 1:3), "down" into a ship (1:3), "down" into the sides of the ship (1:5), and "down" into the depths of the ocean (2:6). Paul Kidwell observed, "Hell is downhill from where we stand." The far country has a hog pen as the sinner's motel (Luke 15). He who once yields to do wrong will find it harder the next time to do right. If sin is harbored in a house, a curse waits at the door, like a bailiff, ready to arrest the sinner whenever he looks out (cf. Achan's family, Joshua 7:1).

Moses told the leaders of the two and half tribes: "Be sure your sin will find you out" (Numbers 32:23; cf. Genesis 44:16; Psalm 139:11-12). The emphasis is upon *you*. The language points to a man's sin avenging itself, tracking down its victim and demanding its pound of flesh. "He that sinneth against me wrongeth his own soul" (Proverbs 8:36), Wisdom said. There is no escape from it. "Woe unto the wicked! It shall be ill with him; for the reward of his hands shall be given him" (Isaiah 3:11).

In Cain's case, he ignored God's warning, walked out the door, and was attacked by the vicious animal. For the first time in the history of mankind, sin painted man's face with the dark colors of hatred and jealousy. Hate lifted its hand and Cain committed the first murder; the blood of Abel cried for vengeance from the ground (Genesis 4:10), stained for the first time with the blood of man.

In contrast to sin's stalking of a sinner, God pleads with a sinner. God reasoned with Cain, trying to get him to see his sin and foolishness (cf. Isaiah 1:18). He sets before him death and a curse, but also life and blessing (cf. Deuteronomy 30:15, 19). He hopes Cain will cool his anger and prevent the sins that anger will bring into his life. Here we see God's patience in dealing so tenderly with so bad a man, in so bad an affair. "He is not willing that any should perish, but that all should come to repentance" (2 Peter 3:9; cf. Luke 15:28; Ezekiel 18:25). Notice how early in history "the gospel" was preached, and forgiveness is offered to a sinner.

Have you eaten the wormy apple? Have you been visited by the thief?

Have you be attacked by the predator? *Get rid of your sins!* God's wonderful grace has a plan for non-Christians (faith, John 3:16; repentance, Luke 13:3; confession of Christ, Matthew 10:32; baptism, Acts 2:38) and Christians (repentance, confession, prayer, Acts 8:22; James 5:16). *Get rid of your guilt!* Once God has forgotten your sins, do yourself a favor; forget them as well. "For if our heart condemn us, God is greater than our heart, and knoweth all things. Beloved, if our heart condemn us not, then have we confidence toward God" (1 John 3:20-21).

This will cure your sickness and restore the innocence to your soul, the comfort to your pillow, the confidence to your eye, and the influence to your life.

Discussion Questions

1. Did sin turn out like Eve thought it would? Give some examples of how sin turns out for young people today, contrasted with how they thought it would end.

2. Would it be accurate to refer to sin as "poison"? What verses in this lesson support this answer?

3. Would you sit in a chair and look down the shotgun barrel mentioned in this chapter? What are some ways young people do something similar?

4. What is God's cure for a sin-sick soul?

5. Describe how a guilty person feels when the burden of sin is removed by Christ's blood.

6. What are some of the things sin can steal from a young person? (Feel free to list additional ones from those mentioned.)

7. Pick one of the sins listed on the chart on page 12 to discuss further. Contrast how a Christian's viewpoint of the same activity differs so much from popular culture.

8. What do you think the Bible means when it says: "There is no peace, saith the LORD, unto the wicked" (Isaiah 48:22)?

9. How important is it for a teen/college student to keep a good reputation? What are some ways one can tarnish his/her reputation?

10. What are some ways the Bible pictures temptation?

11. Give both a Bible and a current example of this truth: "Be sure your sins will find you out" (Numbers 22:32).

12. Explain the two key concepts in this verse, "He is not willing that any should perish, but that all should come to repentance" (2 Peter 3:9).

CHAPTER 2

BIRDS OF A FEATHER

Lesson text: 1 Samuel 18:1–9
Memory verse: "A man that hath friends must shew himself friendly: and there is a friend that sticketh closer than a brother" (Proverbs 18:24).

Recently I received a letter from a young man we baptized last year. He is in jail and facing the probability of remaining there for several years. He wrote to ask the church to forgive him, and he told a familiar story of getting caught with marijuana and drug paraphernalia. He asked me to tell the young people in the church to *be careful who they choose to hang out with.* So I did last Sunday, and now I am in this chapter.

Peer pressure is a strong force at any age, but it is especially strong among teens who are still forming their values. Peer pressure can be bad; a poisonous apple offered by a friend is much more attractive than one offered by an obvious enemy. But peer pressure can also be good. Godly friends help one another resist temptation.

Let's look at the story of David and Jonathan and learn the lessons of godly friendship.

A FRIENDSHIP BORN (READ 1 SAMUEL 18:1-5)

After David killed Goliath, things started happening pretty fast in his life. He had left his father's house on a simple errand to check on his brothers and take them supplies. He probably wore his usual shepherd's clothes and planned to be home in time to sleep in his own bed that night. But when he arrived at the battlefield, he ended up fighting the giant nobody else would fight—killing him, becoming a hero, and being drafted into Saul's army—all in one day! Saul was so captivated by David that he took him home with him (18:2)—when you're a king, you can do that (1 Samuel 8:11). Since David had shown more courage than Saul's soldiers by fighting Goliath, Saul set him over them (1 Samuel 18:5).

The friendship of Jonathan and David was based on mutual admiration and trust. Imagine the first time Jonathan saw David as David returned from battle with Goliath's bloody head in his hand (1 Samuel 17:57). How he must have admired his courage! At that time, "the soul of Jonathan was knit with the soul of David" (1 Samuel 18:1); that is, they became instant friends. Someone has said "a friend is another self," and these two men seemed to have one soul in two bodies.

Jonathan and David had similar likes, goals, and hopes and were near the same age. The king's son was courageous, popular, and handsome. David had shown courage in fighting Goliath, which led to popularity, and he had already been described as, "ruddy . . . of a beautiful countenance, and goodly to look to" (1 Samuel 16:12). They had common experiences. Jonathan had attacked a Philistine garrison with the same faith and bravery with which David had attacked the giant (1 Samuel 14; 17). But they came from different backgrounds, since David was a poor shepherd and Jonathan a king's son, which shows that friendships can cross external barriers if there is much in common on a spiritual level.

The key in any relationship is trust. David would soon come to trust Jonathan with his life—literally. For one to be the kind of friend he should be, he must be willing to open up and "knit" his soul with another person. This is not always easy because opening up means we may get hurt, but it is necessary. The rewards are worth the risks (Proverbs 27:6).

Our friendships should be based upon mutual admiration. Some try to buy friends with presents or by always paying for meals, snacks, and entertainment, but as George D. Prentice said, "A friend you have to buy won't be worth what you pay for him." That friendship will last only as long as the money does—if that long. Instead, pick someone who respects you for who you are and someone you can respect for who he or she is. The Bible says Jonathan "delighted" in David (1 Samuel 19:2). This Hebrew verb describes "laughter, enjoyment, and pleasure." They had a good time together!

Their friendship was based on their common faith in God. They were both heroic warriors, but their bravery was based in a trust that God would help them. Notice these similar statements they made before they ever even met each other. Jonathan said before attacking the Philistines, "Come, and let us go over unto the garrison of these uncircumcised: it may be that the Lord will work for us: for there is no restraint to the Lord to save by many or by few" (1 Samuel 14:6). When David attacked Goliath, he said, "All this assembly shall know that the Lord saveth not with sword and spear: for the battle is the Lord's, and he will give you into our hands" (1 Samuel 17:47).

Their friendship was based on brotherly love. "And Jonathan loved him as his own soul" (1 Samuel 18:1, 3). According to the Bible, loving someone includes looking out for his or her best interests (1 Corinthians 13:5). Jonathan did that for David. He protected David from Saul, even though he understood that David would be anointed king instead of him. Many teens think love exists only between males and females—and that is a wonderful experience—but men can deeply love each other as friends, and women can have that kind of love for each other. David later said at Jonathan's funeral: "Thy love was wonderful to me, passing the love of women" (2 Samuel 1:26). There is nothing to suggest any homosexual perversion in David and Jonathan (cf. Romans 1:24–28). Each was a "man's man" (athletic warrior) and "God's man" (holy). Both married and fathered children. There is no hint of any abnormality; they had brotherly love.

Friends can enjoy athletics and recreation together. They can work and socialize together. But they can do more than that. They can talk about deep subjects and trust each other to understand and keep conversations private.

Many young women are better at this than young men. Men often have numerous acquaintances but few friends, lots of associates but few companions. As a result, they can feel lonely, isolated, and misunderstood. Aristotle said, "He who has many friends, has none." To have friends, one must be willing to love—to put another's interests ahead of his own (Philippians 2:3).

Their friendship involved sharing. "Jonathan stripped himself of the robe that was upon him, and gave it to David, and his garments, even to his sword, and to his bow, and to his girdle" (1 Samuel 18:4). Jonathan took one look at David and knew he couldn't go to the palace dressed like that! David was a peasant boy, and had not even had a chance to return home, so he did not have clothes befitting his new public life. Jonathan, the king's son, gave him his own clothes. (They were probably the best money could buy.) David was armed only with a shepherd's weapons, so Jonathan, the soldier, gave him a sword and bow. This showed great generosity, as these were treasured items not casually surrendered.

Their friendship was held together by a verbal contract (1 Samuel 18:3). It was not enough that "the soul of Jonathan was knit to the soul of David"—they wanted to seal their friendship with a formal commitment. An African proverb says: "Hold a true friend with both your hands." Jonathan and David formed a covenant in which each promised to support and protect the other. This was so important to them that they later twice renewed it (1 Samuel 20:14–17; 23:16–18). The second time Jonathan said, "Let the Lord even require it" (20:16), which means, "Let the Lord hold David accountable for this covenant's obligations." David agreed to show kindness not only to Jonathan, but also to his descendants.

A FRIENDSHIP STRENGTHENED IN THE LORD
(READ 1 SAMUEL 23:16)

The last time Jonathan and David ever saw each other, as far as the Bible records, Jonathan searched out his friend and "strengthened his hand in God" (1 Samuel 23:16; cf. Nehemiah 2:18). This friendship had always included the Lord (1 Samuel 20:12–13, 23, 42), and now Jonathan built on that foundation to encourage his downtrodden friend not to lose his faith. There is not a single person who does not need encouraging once in a while. Even David—the hero of the Goliath battle—felt his faith growing weak after all of Saul's mistreatment. Jonathan sensed it and encouraged him not to give up. What he said is not recorded. He may have quoted Scripture or prayed a prayer. Whatever he said, David was stronger when he left.

Each should encourage those around him to be more like Christ (1 Peter 2:21–22). This can be done by inviting others to worship and other spiritual activities (John 1:41–42), teaching non-Christians the gospel (Acts 24:25), and talking with those who are tempted to sin (Acts 11:23). Invite non-Christian friends to study the Bible (2 Timothy 2:15) and pray with Christian friends (Acts 20:36).

When the books are balanced in heaven, Jonathan will get quite a bit of credit for David's success. David was at the point of losing his faith. If he had lost it, he would never have become king. Why did Jonathan not say, "If David fails, it is no fault of mine. If he fails, it will only mean that he will not take away the throne that belongs to me." Jonathan and David were friends, and that mattered more to him than being a king. Sure, Jonathan lost a crown, but he won a friend. He threw aside the crown that he might have worn for a little while for a crown he will wear forever.

WHAT ABOUT FRIENDS TODAY?

The best Old Testament example of friendship is Jonathan's bond with David. They shared an uncommon friendship rarely equaled. Will you find a friendship like this? Keep this one thought in mind: To have a friend you must be a friend. "A man that hath friends must shew himself friendly" (Proverbs 18:24).

Being friendly means more than smiling and saying hello or even being kind and helpful. Review the qualities of the friendship between Jonathan and David: admiration and trust, faith in God, brotherly love, sharing, and commitment. Isn't that the kind of friend you want to have? Isn't that the kind of friend you want to be?

Discussion questions

1. Why do you think Jonathan and David became such good friends?

2. What is the key to any relationship? How can this trait be gained and maintained?

3. What is required to "knit" our souls with our friends?

4. Discuss how Saul and David handled "abasement" (defeat) and "abounding" (success) when the young women sang, "Saul hath slain his thousands, and David his ten thousands" (1 Samuel 18:7). How does this apply to young people today?

5. What is meant by these statements? Pick one to discuss:
   a. "A friend you have to buy won't be worth what you pay for him."
   b. "He who has many friends, has none."
   c. "Hold a true friend with both your hands."

6. What is a fair-weather friend? How can we avoid being one?

7. Was there any hint of homosexuality in this story? What does God think of homosexuality? (Read Romans 1:24–28.)

8. How important is it to have friends who share your interests in spiritual things and a desire to please God? What are some ways we can make our friendships more spiritually oriented?

9. One of the best talents a friend can have is that of listening. Give some practical ways to develop this ability.

10. What did Jonathan do for David the last time the Bible records that they saw each other? Why is this significant, and how does it apply to friendships today?

11. What do you think Jonathan said to David that encouraged him?

12. How can church youth groups help young Christians make friends?

CHAPTER 3

WATCH OUT FOR BAD APPLES

Lesson text: 2 Samuel 13:1–16 (read or teacher relate the story)
Memory verse: "Be not deceived: evil communications corrupt good manners" (1 Corinthians 15:33).

One important aspect of teen life is friendship. We all need friends, but bad friends are worse than no friends at all. One preacher said,

> Were I asked to name the chief peril of the great city for the young men and the young women who every year pour into it, seeking their careers, I should say, without any hesitation, it is the peril of hastily formed and ill-chosen friendships . . . I wish I could meet every train coming into the city bringing its precious cargo of young lives starting out on the great adventure of the world; that I could encounter every young man as he comes to the doors of college . . . that I could meet them as they throng to shop and factory and office, and as they come back to their . . . houses, and say to them all, "Who is your friend?"

When you move to a new town or school or start a new job, remember that not everyone who acts friendly will be a true friend; some will quickly prove to be false.

FIND A GOOD FRIEND

If you are a normal person, you want friends. Furthermore, you need friends. "God divided man into men," said Seneca, "that they might have friends." A dangerous trend exists in the world of the Internet, video games, and a hundred channels of surround-sound television: Teens tend to block out the world and become loners. It is easy for those who do not fit in easily to choose not to fit in at all. From the beginning of time, God said it is not good to be alone (Genesis 2:18), and that thought applies to more than husbands and wives; most of us need companionship to be happy.

In Acts, and in Paul's letters, we find at least one hundred different men and women named as a part of Paul's circle of friends and fellow laborers. Paul chose friends who shared his spiritual values. Spiritually, we need friends to encourage us in our daily walk with the Lord, and we need to avoid people who would lead us astray.

The Bible says, "Evil communications corrupt good manners" (1 Corinthians 15:33); that is, "Evil company corrupts good habits." Making a close friendship with a "bad apple" (an ungodly person) is spiritually dangerous.

The impressionable minds of young people who are still building strong faith are especially susceptible to negative influence. Those with bad language and rebellious conduct will pressure us to be like them. The wise man said, "Make no friendship with an angry man; and with a furious man thou shalt not go: lest thou learn his ways, and get a snare to thy soul" (Proverbs 22:24–25). Paul instructed,

> Young men likewise exhort to be sober minded. In all things shewing thyself a pattern of good works: in doctrine shewing uncorruptness, gravity, sincerity, sound speech, that cannot be condemned; that he

that is of the contrary part may be ashamed, having no evil thing to say of you (Titus 2:6–8).

Pass on a bad friend

Friendship can be abused. As ocean tides depend on the moon's pull, our behavior depends to a great extent upon the influence others exert on us. Thus we must choose our environment carefully. From the thief and the drunkard to the man who mocks God, nearly every sinner got the suggestion from somebody else. Sinners first breathe tainted atmosphere poisoned by the sins of other men, and thus evil makes its way to their hearts, much like physical disease spreads from one person to another through physical contact.

Amnon: A case study

Amnon was a very disturbed son of David. He developed an ungodly sexual desire toward his own half-sister, Tamar (2 Samuel 13:2). God placed significant obstacles between Amnon and sin:

- » His conscience registered an objection;
- » Her innocence made him pause ("she was a virgin; and Amnon thought it hard for him to do any thing to her");
- » Her pleading and reasoning appealed to his pity;
- » The threat of his father's anger and his brother's revenge made him fearful;
- » He knew that God would judge him (2 Corinthians 5:10).

In short, Amnon knew better, but he still succumbed to temptation and committed the brutal deed. "Howbeit he would not hearken unto her voice: but, being stronger than she, forced her, and lay with her" (2 Samuel 13:14). He raped his own sister.

Amnon, however, was not the only guilty person in this crime. Let's skip ahead a couple of years. As Amnon sat half-drunk at a feast with his half-brother, Absalom's servant ended Amnon's life (2 Samuel 13:29). The sin-laden soul was hurried into eternity to stand before its Maker. Only Amnon died that day, but another man, Jonadab, also deserved to die. If he had not aided, abetted, and arranged the scheme, Amnon would not have defiled his sister. The man who helped him start down sin's path was not there when he came to its end.

The beginning of the end started with these words: "But Amnon had a friend, whose name was Jonadab" (2 Samuel 13:3). The Bible describes him as "subtle," which means "crafty" or "shrewd." Jonadab's method of persuading Amnon is still popular. When Amnon confided his desire but also his hesitation, Jonadab said, "Are you not a king's son?" He implied that the king's son should have whatever he wants.

When we stand near a temptation and our conscience frowns at us, when our Bible teachers' lessons run through our minds, and when our parents' love and trust hold us back, a subtle friend may appear who whispers tauntingly, "Are you not a king's son?" (Actually he says, "You're not frightened by a Sunday school lesson about hell, are you? Your mommy's not here. Be a man!")

Wherever a soul perishes, somewhere there lurks a tempter, a Jonadab, a false friend. Test your friends before they ruin you. No bad person can be a good friend. The teen that has not firmly made up his or her mind about what is right and wrong will be easily influenced by companions. A person who has not chosen a direction—a goal—may be easily led down the wrong path.

Separation from evil influences is one way God keeps His children holy. Paul wrote,

> Be ye not unequally yoked together with unbelievers: for what fellowship hath righteousness with unrighteousness? and what communion hath light with darkness? And what concord hath Christ with Belial? or what part hath he that believeth with an infidel? And what agreement hath the temple of God with idols? for ye are the temple of the living God; as God hath said, I will dwell in them, and

walk in them; and I will be their God, and they shall be my people. Wherefore come out from among them, and be ye separate, saith the Lord, and touch not the unclean thing; and I will receive you, and will be a Father unto you, and ye shall be my sons and daughters, saith the Lord Almighty (2 Corinthians 6:14–18).

Instead of letting others influence you, have such purpose that you influence them. If you must choose between having no friends or having one like Jonadab, choose none. Be determined to have no person for a close friend who will not help you go to heaven. Be your own person!

A true friend leads you toward Christ, not away from Him (Acts 18:26). A true friend builds your faith instead of weakening it. Paul said, "Let us therefore follow after the things which make for peace, and things wherewith one may edify another" (Romans 14:19; cf. 15:2). A true friend helps to keep you from falling away from God. When climbing a mountain, climbers sometimes pair up and rope themselves together, so if one slips the other can pull him back up. Solomon said, "Two are better than one," because a friend will "lift up his fellow: but woe to him that is alone when he falleth; for he hath not another to help him up" (Ecclesiastes 4:9–10).

You will meet many people in your life, and many will say they are your friends. Some, like Jonadab, will tempt you to sin and then desert you, letting you suffer the consequences alone. Others, like Jonathan, will encourage you to serve the Lord and even sacrifice so you can be happy or successful.

Watch out for bad apples. Ask yourself, Jonadab or Jonathan? Choose carefully: more than your life may depend on it.

Discussion Questions

1. What are some characteristics of people who make good friends? What are some characteristics that keep one from being a good friend?

2. What are some ways to show yourself friendly (Proverbs 18:24) and gain more friends? What ways should not be tried?

3. Why is making a close friendship with a "bad apple" (an ungodly person) spiritually dangerous? (Proverbs 22:24–25).

4. What is the danger of hiding ourselves behind technology and avoiding social contact and friends?

5. What obstacles stood between Amnon and the sin that he was tempted to commit? Which of these obstacles stands between us and sin today? What other things can we do to avoid sin?

6. What role did Jonadab play in Amnon's sin? Where was Jonadab when the consequences of Amnon's sin caught up to Amnon?

7. Discuss how this passage applies to friendship: "Be ye not unequally yoked together with unbelievers" (2 Corinthians 6:14).

8. Instead of letting others influence us to sin, what should we do to them?

CHAPTER 4

DON'T TRIP OVER YOUR TONGUE ON THE WAY TO HEAVEN

Lesson text: James 3:1–12
Memory verse: "Wherefore, my beloved brethren, let every man be swift to hear, slow to speak, slow to wrath" (James 1:19).

Stephen Pile told of a man who lit a fire in his grate and went outside to get more coal. Upon returning, he noted that a log had rolled out of the grate and set the log box on fire. He picked up the burning box and hurried to throw it out into his yard. As he did, he brushed the curtain that covered the front door.

Upon returning, he noted that the curtain and the door were in flames. While phoning the fire station, he also noticed that the log box he had thrown out into the yard had set fire to his car. He rushed out with a bucket of water, but in the process, he tripped over a gasoline can which splashed gas on him and the surrounding area. By then a neighbor had called the fire station. By the time the firemen arrived, they found the entire place aflame, including the man who started it all; he was trying to leap out of his clothes.

A fire usually begins with a small spark like a match or an ember in the wrong place. In the same way, the wrong word can spark an emotional fire that becomes a raging, uncontrolled agent of destruction we never intended. We should heed God's advice to be "slow to speak" (James 1:19). Abraham Lincoln delivered the Gettysburg Address over 140 years ago. Look at how his words compare with other kinds of communication:

	Number of words
Gettysburg Address	272
Bag of Lay's Potato Chips	401
IRS Form 1040 EZ	418
Average *USA Today* cover story	1,200

The average teen speaks enough in one week to fill a 500-page book. In the average lifetime, that would be 3,000 volumes. Thus the average person uses 26,800 words a day. That's 9,782,000 words a year and 733,650,000 words in a lifetime of 75 years.

Do we really need to use that many words? A wise person learns that the quality of one's words is more important than the quantity. The Declaration of Independence used only 1,821 words. Moses used only 400 words to describe the creation of the world. God used only 297 words to give the Ten Commandments.

Someone said, "He who thinks by the inch and talks by the yard will likely be moved by the foot." Many of the words people choose bring no glory to God and do no good for man. We should be "slow to speak" (James 1:19).

WHY WATCH YOUR WORDS?

Words can ruin our religion (James 1:26). A bad mouth can ruin our reputation with others and our standing with God. Thomas Fuller said, "Birds are entangled by their feet and men by their tongues." We must bridle the tongue with self-control before others bridle it for us. "Be ye not as the horse, or as the mule, which have no understanding: whose mouth must be held in with bit and bridle, lest they come near unto thee" (Psalm 32:9). A sentence may seem like a small thing, but it can lead to big results.

A squirrel climbed on the Metro-North Railroad power lines near New York City. This set off an electrical surge, which weakened an overhead bracket, which let a wire dangle toward the tracks, which tangled in a train, which tore down all the lines. As a result, 47,000 commuters were stuck in Manhattan for hours. Such a small cause had such a big effect. James teaches us that one of the smallest parts of the body—the tongue—can cause a lot of damage (James 3:5–6).

Words can lead to condemnation (James 3:1–2). Solomon said, "He that keepeth his mouth keepeth his life: but he that openeth wide his lips shall have destruction" (Proverbs 13:3). Benjamin Franklin said, "A slip of the foot you may soon recover, but a slip of the tongue you may never get over."

Words may have to be eaten. David's son said, "Death and life are in the power of the tongue: and they that love it shall eat the fruit thereof" (Proverbs 18:21). Be careful with words, for they have consequences. Just five words cost Zacharias nine months of silence (Luke 1:20).

Words put us in danger of sinning. Chaucer wrote, "The first virtue, son, if you will learn, is to restrain and keep well thy tongue." Solomon said, "In the multitude of words there wanteth [lacketh] not sin: but he that refraineth his lips is wise" (Proverbs 10:19). Since the tongue is capable of many sins, the more we use it, the more likely we are to sin. Someone noted, "God gave two ears which are always open and one tongue surrounded by two rows of teeth, which should give some indication as to what He intended." Both Diogenes and Zeno are credited with saying, "We have two ears and only one tongue in order that we may hear more and speak less." Another observed, "Even a fish would stay out of trouble if he kept his mouth shut."

Perhaps the tongue is second only to the hand in the number of sins it can commit. The Bible lists at least fifteen sins we can commit with our tongue:

1. Taking God's name in vain. "Thou shalt not take the name of the Lord thy God in vain; for the Lord will not hold him guiltless that taketh his name in vain" (Exodus 20:7). God's name is taken in vain by using it flippantly.

Some people use God's name in everyday speech without thinking at all about what they are saying. Some hear bad news and exclaim, "My God!" Another arrives at an accident scene and utters, "Christ! What happened here?"

Someone wrote,

> You may sport with the whirlwind and trifle with the storm; you may lay your hand upon the lion's mane and play with the leopard's spots; you may go to the very crater of the burning volcano and laugh at the lava which it belches out in thunder. You may trifle with any and everything, but trifle not with God. Let there be one holy thing upon which you dare not lay a profane hand, and let that be the name of God (*The Biblical Illustrator*, p. 359).

God's name is taken in vain by using euphemisms. Many who would never think of using holy names as interjections will nonetheless use euphemisms. An interjection is an "ejaculatory word or form of speech, usually thrown in without grammatical connection" (*Webster's Dictionary*). A euphemism is "the substitution of a word or phrase less offensive or objectionable."

Many young people have allowed words to creep into their vocabularies that should not be there. They would be shocked if they knew their origin. Some common euphemisms include the following:

» "Lordy" or "Lawe me," refer to the Lord;
» "Gee Whiz," "Jeez," or "Gee," euphemistic contractions of the name of Jesus;
» "Gosh, Golly, Gad, Egad," for God.
» "Good gracious," "Good grief," "My Goodness," "Goodness knows," "For Goodness sake," and "Thank Goodness," mild oaths that euphemistically refer to God;
» "Heavens," "Good heavens," and "For heaven's sake" call on heaven to witness the truth (cf. Matthew 23:22).
» "Darn," "Dang," "Dern," simply mean "damn."

- » "Dickens" and "Deuce" refer to the devil.
- » "Heck" means hell.

(References: *Webster's New World Dictionary*, *Webster's Unabridged Dictionary*, *American English Usage*, *Nicholson*, *Funk & Wagnalls Practical Dictionary*, *Webster's New Intercollegiate Dictionary*).

2. Cursing/Profanity (Exodus 22:28; James 3:10; 2 Peter 2:10; Jude 1:8). Cursing is widespread. Television and movies fill scripts with four-letter words. Fiction writers can't seem to write a page without profanity. Presidents have been known to curse both on and off camera. Some people delight in peppered speech so much that they appear to exhale and inhale curse words like a fish does water. "Pure Speech and Profanity," a popular tract by Garland Elkins and Stoy Pate, comments on the common usage of bad language in our culture:

> [People] swear when they are mad and when they are glad; when they are satisfied and when they are disappointed; when they are fortunate, and when they are unfortunate; when they are sick, and when they are well; when they are blessed in work or play, in earnest and in fun, and for a thousand other reasons (Getwell church of Christ, Memphis, Tennessee. 1977. p. 6).

Paul Harvey said, "Profanity is insanity." It is a prayer to God to carry out a curse of revenge, but Jesus said to love our enemies (Matthew 5:44; Romans 12:14). We are to love our neighbor, not curse our neighbor (Matthew 22:39). God wants all to be saved and not to be doomed (1 Timothy 2:4; Ezekiel 33:11; 2 Peter 3:9). We should never wish others to be damned—we should wish them to be saved (cf. Mark 16:16).

Profanity is evidence of an evil heart (Matthew 12:34). As a table of contents tells what one will find in a book, so speech tells others what they will find in our hearts. When Peter wanted to convince the Jews that he did not know Jesus, he began to curse and swear (Matthew 26:72–74). Cursing has the same effect today. God even wants us to stay away from those who curse (Proverbs 29:24; Ephesians 5:11). Cursing keeps us from God's blessings (Psalm 109:17).

Someone has written a tongue-in-cheek reminder of the foolishness of swearing by collecting the "Ten Reasons Why I Swear":

1. It pleases Mother so much.
2. It is a fine mark of manliness.
3. It proves I have self-control.
4. It indicates how clearly my mind operates.
5. It makes my conversation so pleasing to everybody.
6. It leaves no doubt in anyone's mind as to my good breeding.
7. It impresses people that I have more than ordinary education.
8. It is an unmistakable sign of culture and refinement.
9. It makes me very desirable personally among women and children.
10. It is my way of honoring God who said, "Thou shalt not take the name of the Lord thy God in vain."

3. Flattery (Psalm 12:2–3). It is good to compliment, but it is sinful to flatter. Jesus never flattered anyone, but He did compliment five people. He said that Nathaniel was one "in whom is no guile" (John 1:47). Of the Roman centurion He said, "I have not found so great faith, no not in Israel" (Matthew 8:5–10). Of His cousin, John the Baptist, He said, "Among them that are born of women there hath not risen a greater than John the Baptist" (Matthew 11:11). He complimented a poor widow on her giving (Mark 12:41–44). He complimented the woman who anointed His feet with costly oil and wiped them with her hair (John 12:1–8). Thus Jesus complimented people for honesty, faith, fearless preaching, liberality, and doing good works.

On the other hand, Jesus never flattered. Others tried to flatter Him (Matthew 22:16), but He never did the same. To have done so would have been to violate the Old Testament and His own law. "A man that flattereth his neighbour spreadeth a net for his feet" (Proverbs 29:5; cf. 20:19; 26:28; 28:23). Job resisted the temptation of flattery (Job 17:5; 32:22). Paul never "at any time used . . . flattering words" (1 Thessalonians 2:5). We must give care to avoid this form of sinful speech.

4. **Evil speaking/Frowardness** (Ephesians 4:31; James 4:11; Proverbs 4:24; 8:8, 13; 1 Timothy 6:5; 1 Peter 2:1). Paul wrote, "Let your speech be always with grace, seasoned with salt, that ye may know how ye ought to answer every man" (Colossians 4:6). "Keep thy tongue from evil, and thy lips from speaking guile" (Psalm 34:13).

5. **Lying/Deceit** (Revelation 21:8; Proverbs 6:17–19; Romans 3:13; Ephesians 4:25). The ninth commandment says, "Thou shalt not bear false witness against thy neighbor" (Exodus 20:16). Edgar J. Hohn in an old issue of *Reader's Digest* observed, "A lie has speed, but truth has endurance." Solomon said, "Better is the poor that walketh in his integrity, than he that is perverse in his lips, and is a fool" (Proverbs 19:1).

6. **Talebearing** (Proverbs 26:20). Gossip is dangerous (Proverbs 20:19; 11:13; 2 Corinthians 12:20) because it wounds (Proverbs 18:8, 21; Psalm 41:7), separates friends (Proverbs 17:9; 16:28), sows strife and digs up evil (Proverbs 16:27), ensnares the gossiper's own soul (Proverbs 18:7), and is classed with the worst of evils (Romans 1:28–32). According to the National Opinion Research Center, 29 percent of adults say their privacy has been violated by gossiping neighbors (cited in *American Demographics*, 1995).

Someone collected these thoughts on rumors:

» There is nothing as effective as a bunch of facts to spoil a good rumor.

» There's a new margarine on the market named RUMOR—because it spreads so quickly and easily.

» A rumor is about as hard to unspread as butter.

7. **Harsh criticism/Reviling** (Matthew 5:22; 1 Corinthians 6:10). A good statement to remember is, "To belittle is to be little." One woman committed suicide and left an unfinished note that simply said, "They said . . . ."

Whatever "they said" had bothered her enough that she thought life was not any longer worth living.

One can never whitewash himself by slinging mud at another. He who tries only gets his hands dirty. It doesn't hurt to be kind. It may not always be easy to be nice, but it is worth the effort. As Christians, we need to be very sensitive to the needs and feelings of others.

One noted that if you call a lady an old hen, you're in trouble, but she doesn't mind being referred to as a "chick." Tell her she looks like a "breath of spring" instead of "the end of a hard winter." Although it may mean the same thing, it is better to say, "Time stands still when I look into your eyes," than to say, "You have a face that would stop a clock." It matters what we say and how we say it.

8. Whispering (Romans 1:29). On a windswept hill in an English country churchyard stands a drab, gray slate tombstone. Bleak and unpretentious, it leans slightly to one side, beaten slick and thin by the blast of time. The quaint stone bears an epitaph not easily seen unless you stoop over and look closely . . . the faint etching reads,

> *Beneath this stone, a lump of clay,*
> *Lies Arabella Young*
> *Who, on the 24th day of May*
> *Began to hold her tongue.*

Don't be like Arabella; learn to control your speech while you still have a choice!

9. Boasting (Romans 1:30). Some young people are constantly talking about themselves and what they have done or think they can do. Whatever we have done is simply because God gave us the ability and opportunity to do it. Therefore, He alone deserves the praise and glory (Matthew 5:14–16).

10. Backbiting (Psalm 15:1–3; Romans 1:30; Galatians 5:15). All biting is not done with the teeth. Some is done with the tongue, and, compared to teeth, the tongue is sharper (Psalm 57:4). A backbiter is not a person who bites back, but one who bites behind the back. A backbiter is a person with "back trouble." *Backbite* means, "to say a mean or spiteful thing about one absent: to slander." The Hebrew word suggests the idea of "to play the spy." Backbiters keep bad company (Romans 1:29–31) and start church troubles (2 Corinthians 12:20). If a backbiter comes near us, the Bible tells us to give them a dirty look—literally! (Proverbs 25:23).

11. Speaking idle words/foolish talking (Matthew 12:36; cf. 1 Timothy 5:13; Ephesians 5:4). A farmer came to town one day and asked the owner of a restaurant if he could use a million frog legs. The owner asked where he could get that many frogs. "I've got a pond at home just full of them," the farmer replied. "They drive me crazy night and day." After they made an agreement for several hundred frogs, the farmer went back home. He came back a week later with two scrawny frogs and a foolish look on his face. "I guess I was wrong," he stammered. "There were just two frogs in the pond, but they sure were making a lot of noise." The next time you hear a lot of noise about how bad things are at church or in the youth group, just remember it may be nothing more than a couple of complainers who have a negative attitude and like to talk.

12. Filthy speech/jesting (Colossians 3:8; Ephesians 5:4). Paul wrote, "Let no corrupt communication proceed out of your mouth, but that which is good to the use of edifying, that it may minister grace unto the hearers" (Ephesians 4:29). "No corrupt communication" means "not even a little bit, not even when you're angry, not even when you're with the guys, not even when you stump your toe."

13. False teaching (Titus 1:10–11). Have you ever considered that the devil has more preachers and youth leaders on his side than God does? (Read 2 Corinthians 2:11; 11:14.)

14. Blasphemy (Colossians 3:8; cf. Psalm 119:20; Matthew 12:24–37; Mark 3:28–30; Luke 11:14–26; Leviticus 24:16). In an obscure Old Testament passage, there is the record of an Israelite woman who married an Egyptian. Her son got into an argument with an Israelite during the time they were camped near Mount Sinai. During this fight, he blasphemed the name of God and cursed. They brought him before Moses and waited for word from the Lord on what to do to him. "Stone him," was the Lord's answer (Leviticus 24:10–16, 23). This is the first instance in the Bible of one breaking the third of the Ten Commandments.

We, too, must resist the temptation to use God's name irreverently, since God still holds this as a serious sin. We must avoid jokes or stories which rob God of the sacredness and dignity He deserves (cf. Ezekiel 22:26; Ephesians 5:4; Matthew 12:36–37). When facing grief, disappointment, or bitterness, some people blame God and even curse Him (cf. Proverbs 30:8–9). Job's wife urged him to "curse God, and die" (Job 2:9). To his credit, Job refused (1:22; 2:10).

15. Frivolous oath-taking (Leviticus 19:12; Deuteronomy 23:21; Matthew 5:33–37). People make statements like, "As surely as God lives, I will . . ."; Or, "By God, you just watch me;" or, "Just as surely as there is a God in heaven, I'm telling the truth." This is taking the Lord's name in vain. We should keep our promises without having to invoke God's name (Ecclesiastes 5:4). There is no need to seal a promise with an oath, because a Christian's word is his bond. It appears that this prohibition is not against all oath-taking, but against frivolous ones (cf. Matthew 26:63–64; Galatians 1:20; 2 Corinthians 1:23; Philippians 1:8).

Here is a meaningful poem that captures the importance of not tripping over our tongues on the way to heaven:

> "The boneless tongue, so small and weak,
> Can crush and kill," declares the Greek.
> "The tongue destroys a greater horde,"
> The Turk asserts, "than does the sword."
> The Persian proverb wisely saith,
> "A lengthy tongue—an early death!"

Or sometimes takes this form instead,
"Don't let your tongue cut off your head."
"The tongue can speak a word whose speed,"
Say the Chinese, "outstrips the steed."
The Arab sages said in part,
"The tongue's great storehouse is the heart."
From Hebrew was the maxim sprung,
"Thy feet should slip, but ne'er the tongue."
The sacred writer crowns the whole,
"Who keeps the tongue doth keep his soul."

Discussion Questions

1. What two parts of the body can likely commit the most sins? Discuss.
   a. Eyes and feet
   b. Mind and ears
   c. Hands and mouth
   d. Gall bladder and spleen

2. How do the following Scriptures apply to the typical teen gathering?
   a. "In the multitude of words there wanteth [lacketh] not sin."
   b. "He that refraineth his lips is wise" (Proverbs 10:19).
   c. "Death and life are in the power of the tongue."
   d. "They that love it shall eat the fruit thereof" (Proverbs 18:21).

3. If one of your Christian friends has gotten into the habit of taking God's name in vain, how would you suggest he or she break the habit?

4. What are some practical ways to avoid getting caught up in the culture of using profanity to fit in or to make a point?

5. Since both flattery and unkindness are sins, discuss how to avoid both when a friend asks your opinion about her clothes or his performance or something else that puts you in danger of doing one or the other.

6. Who do teens lie to the most: parents, teachers, each other, boy/girl friends, strangers? How do you handle it when someone wants you to lie for him/her?

7. Have you ever been hurt by gossip? Have you ever hurt someone's feelings by spreading gossip? What lessons did you learn from the experience?

8. What traits did Jesus compliment in others?

9. Which sin is practiced the most by teens: boasting or backbiting? How is someone who boasts perceived by his/her peers? How is someone who backbites perceived by his/her peers? How does this compare to how God feels about these actions?

10. What is the best way to handle someone telling you an off-color or dirty joke?
    a. Listen and laugh so you don't hurt the person's feelings.
    b. Write it down so you can tell it to your other friends later.
    c. Explain that you don't like those kind of jokes because you are a Christian.
    d. Preach them a sermon in front of everybody about having a dirty mouth.
    e. Another approach (explain to your teacher and class).

CHAPTER 5

GIVE YOUR TOBACCO TO A BILLY GOAT

Lesson text: Romans 6:11–18

Memory verse: "What? know ye not that your body is the temple of the Holy Ghost which is in you, which ye have of God, and ye are not your own?" (1 Corinthians 6:19).

Many children love to sing the old VBS song that says, "Please don't smoke, please don't smoke, give your tobacco to a billy goat."

But you are not a kid anymore, even though some adults still treat you like one. You are a teenager, perhaps even a college student. You now know that your parents don't know everything. You've got a life. You have friends. You spend a good bit of time away from your parents, and you make a lot of decisions that they don't directly influence.

Are you going to start smoking? It's a decision that you will have to make. More than 6,000 people under the age of eighteen years will try their first cigarette today.[1]

The American Lung Association estimates that every minute, 4,800 teens take their first drag off a cigarette. Of those 4,800, about 2,000 will go on to become chain-smokers.[2]

While adult smoking rates have decreased, teen smoking rates are increasing.

About one out of four teens smoke by high school graduation.[3] Two thousand teens[4] will become addicted today—almost 800,000 this year. Most smokers start in their mid-teens and are addicted by the time they graduate from high school. But many kids are smoking by the time they are eleven years old and are addicted by the age of fourteen. Approximately 4.5 million adolescents in the United States are smokers. Getting the cigarettes is no problem for most (although coming up with the money may be) because plenty of businesses don't ask for IDs, and lots of older friends will buy them for others.[5]

I'm not writing this chapter to treat you like a child. I know you have a mind and can make a thoughtful decision. I'm not going to patronize you. In all likelihood we have never met, and perhaps we never will. I won't know if you read this or if you decided pro or con on cigarettes. But you should be aware that this particular "apple" has a very dangerous "worm." Smoking quickly becomes a habit that affects every part of your life. I don't believe you should start smoking. Here's why.

Smoking seems cool, but it makes you stink

Because authority figures, like parents and teachers, warn against smoking, teens naturally want to try it. It appeals to the normal teen flirtation with rebellion to want to do it and shows that their parents don't control them. If they do something that the government says will kill them, then they must be brave. If society says teens are not old enough to buy cigarettes, then smoking makes them look mature. So to some teens, smoking is cool.

The truth is it is not cool. Smoking gives you bad breath and makes your clothes, car, and room stink. One funny thing about this is that most smokers don't even know they stink. They lost most of their sense of smell when they started smoking. Because they are around the stale smell all the time, they don't notice it at all.

They brush their teeth in the morning and may use mouthwash and mints during the day, but from the day's first cigarette, they have smoker's breath. Camel beats out Colgate. Winston is more powerful than Scope. They put on cologne or perfume, but it's overpowered by the scent of smoke. Marlboro overpowers Axe. They wash their clothes, but they don't smell clean—the scent of Kool is stronger than that of Tide.

Bad odor is not cool. No one wants what was true of Lazarus to be said of them: "He stinketh" (John 11:39). Job suffered from breath that was "corrupt" (Job 19:17), but he could not help it. Smoking is a bad idea because it makes you stink.

Smoking is fun, but it makes it harder to get a date

Smoking is enjoyable; otherwise, people would never start and would be able to stop. There is a social price for smoking, though. In a recent teen survey, about three-fourths of high school seniors said they prefer to date someone who doesn't smoke.[6] For many teenagers, taking 75 percent of the available dates off the market doesn't improve the chances of their getting a decent boyfriend or girlfriend.

Why don't teens want to date a smoker? Face it: If you ride in a smoker's car, you are going to smell like smoke. And who wants to be on a date with someone who has bad breath? Most smokers have yellow teeth and three times more cavities[7] than other teens, no matter how often they brush and floss. They often have red eyes and yellow fingers. Smoking is also expensive, so the money to eat at a good restaurant or to do something memorable is less likely to be there if cigarettes are in the pocket.

Dating is one of the joys of youth, but it is also one of the most stressful activities. Finding someone you want to date who wants to date you is not easy for most teens. The Bible talks about both the joys and stresses of courtship. Solomon thought one of the most amazing sights on earth was "the way of a man with a maid" (Proverbs 30:19).

The love story of Isaac and Rebekah, who was "very fair to look upon" (Genesis 24:16), inspires us as we see the joy that awaits the person who finds the right partner. The story of Jacob and Rachel reminds us that love is wonderfully enjoyable and makes life's burdens lighter. "Jacob loved Rachel ... And Jacob served seven years for Rachel; and they seemed unto him but a few days, for the love he had to her" (Genesis 29:18–20). Don't let smoking keep you from finding the best person for you.

Smoking will get you attention, but it is a gateway to using drugs

Many teens like to get attention, even if it's bad attention. They may feel ignored by parents who are consumed in their careers. Maybe they get lost in the crowd at school, when they can't seem to break into the social clique they want to join.

So they turn to smoking. Smoking gets them noticed. Other teens may think they're cool or brave or mature. But is the attention worth the consequences? There are other ways to get noticed. Cigarettes are what experts call a "gateway drug." The Center for Disease Control (CDC) reports,

> Teen smoking is often an early warning sign of future problems. Teens who smoke are three times as likely as nonsmokers to use alcohol, eight times as likely to use marijuana, and 22 times as likely to use cocaine. Smoking is also associated with numerous other high risk behaviors, including fighting and having unprotected sex.
>
> A report from the Center on Addiction and Substance Abuse at Columbia University stated that there is a consistent relationship between the use of cigarettes and the subsequent use of cannabis, and later to illicit drugs like cocaine. This was true regardless of the age, sex, ethnicity, or race of the individuals involved. Those 12 to 17 years old who smoke are 19 times more likely to use cocaine. The more often teens use cigarettes, the more likely they are to use cocaine, heroin, hallucinogens, and other illicit drugs.[7]

Solomon said, "Ponder the path of thy feet, and let all thy ways be established. Turn not to the right hand nor to the left: remove thy foot from evil" (Proverbs 4:26–27).

Smoking makes you feel good, but it hurts your athletic ability

The nicotine in cigarettes gives a boost to the body. Nicotine is a stimulant, and it gives you a buzz. Within one minute of starting to smoke, the heart rate begins to rise, increasing by as much as 30 percent during the first ten minutes of smoking. First time or irregular users receive an increase in alertness and memory. This psychoactive drug's "high" provides a dopamine "aaahhh" sensation.[9] The immediate effect is a rise in blood pressure, an adrenaline rush, and a feeling of euphoria.

Smoking makes a body feel good, but it is in no sense good for the body. Everybody knows the long-term effects of smoking include cancer, strokes, and lung and heart problems. But what many teens don't know is the damage to the body starts in the short-term.

Cigarettes have about 4000 chemicals in them. Among them are several poisons:

- » Nicotine: a poison used to kill sharks. Drop for drop, it is more lethal than strychnine and three times deadlier than arsenic.
- » Arsenic: used in rat poison.
- » Methane: a component of rocket fuel.
- » Ammonia: found in floor cleaners.
- » Cadmium: used in batteries.
- » Carbon Monoxide: part of car exhaust.
- » Formaldehyde: undertakers use to preserve body tissue.
- » Butane: lighter fluid.
- » Hydrogen Cyanide: the poison used in gas chambers.[10]

Every time one inhales cigarette smoke, small amounts of these chemicals go into the blood through the lungs. They travel to all the parts of the body, causing great harm.

Sports are important during the teen years. The majority of teens play either on a school team, community team, or with friends for fun. Smoking and high-level athletics do not go together. Consider why:

- » Teens who smoke are more likely to get sick than those who don't, and they have a harder time recovering from illness. They are more likely than nonsmokers to get bronchitis and pneumonia. Thus athletes miss practice and games. Their grades can suffer, which hinders getting accepted for college athletic scholarships.

- Teen smokers have smaller lungs and weaker hearts than teen nonsmokers. This is because tobacco slows down lung growth and reduces lung function. Every time smoke is inhaled, some of the lung's air sacs—alveoli—are destroyed. These sacs are where oxygen is transferred into the blood. Since alveoli do not grow back, permanent lung damage starts taking place with the first cigarette.[11] A nineteen-year-old smoker frequently has the lungs of a thirty-year-old nonsmoker.

- Teen smokers suffer from shortness of breath almost three times as often as teens who do not smoke. Of course, this means that you won't do as well in activities where breathing is important, like sports or singing. Small lung capacity leaves one gulping for air when one needs it most.[12] Regardless of the sport, breath is one thing an athlete cannot afford to be short of!

- Nicotine increases heart rate, which complicates the body's ability to maintain homeostasis during exercise. A smoker's heartbeat is three times faster than a nonsmoker. In competition, a smoker's body wastes a lot of heartbeats just trying to keep up with nonsmokers.

- Smoking increases the carbon monoxide level, which adversely affects athletic performance.[13]

- Young smokers produce phlegm more than twice as often as those who do not smoke. This further hinders the breathing process.

- Nicotine makes it harder to control one's nerves. This is a key to performing well in most sports, even those that do not require as much lung capacity.

- Nicotine increases blood pressure by vaso-constriction of peripheral vessels.[14]

Think about it: when is the last time you saw a professional athlete light up? They don't—at least not the ones who last.

The Bible talks about enjoying the strength of youth: "The glory of young men is their strength" (Proverbs 20:29). Solomon instructed, "Rejoice, O young man, in thy youth; and let thy heart cheer thee in the days of thy youth, and walk in the ways of thine heart, and in the sight of thine eyes." Then he adds this sober warning: "But know thou, that for all these things God will bring thee into judgment" (Ecclesiastes 11:9). Don't let cigarettes steal your athletic ability.

Smoking relieves stress, but it hinders getting a good job

The teenage years are stressful. There is pressure to make good grades so you can get into a good college. There is social pressure to fit in and be in a boyfriend/girlfriend relationship. There is pressure associated with competition—athletic, band, and other extracurricular activities. There is family pressure placed on many teens, especially those from divorced, dysfunctional, or drug-dependent, families. There is the pressure to look good and be good.

Some turn to nicotine to ease their nerves, just as some turn to alcohol or other drugs.

This is an expensive cop-out. Since the purpose of going to college is usually to get a good job, starting smoking in high school is counterproductive. Many employers do not like to hire smokers. In fact, employers are coached not to hire smokers:[15] "The proper solution, the legal solution, as voluminous case law shows, is to not hire the foreseeable offenders in the first place."[16] By the time today's teens get to the workforce, the likelihood is that this will be commonplace. It is already taking form. The American Civil Liberties Union's (ACLU) National Workrights Institute estimates that more than 6,000 companies refuse to hire smokers.[17] For example,

» Union Pacific Corporation, an Omaha, Nebraska, based transportation company, stopped hiring smokers in seven states. Company officials said the move was made to help quell employee health costs, which have jumped more than 10 percent each of the past three years.[18]

» The World Health Organization stopped hiring smokers in 2005, as part of its commitment to controlling tobacco use. Applicants are now asked if they smoke or use other tobacco products, and if they answer yes, the application process is terminated.[19]

» Kalamazoo Valley Community College in Michigan stopped hiring smokers for full-time positions at both its Michigan campuses.

» Alaska Airlines, based in Washington State, requires a nicotine test before hiring people.

» The Tacoma-Pierce County (Washington) Health Department has applicants sign an "affidavit of nontobacco use."[20]

» Weyco Inc., an employee benefits company with 200 employees in Okemos, Michigan, takes it a step further.[21] It runs random drug tests for nicotine, firing workers who fail the test or refuse to quit smoking.[22]

Why take such a hard line against hiring smokers? On average, smokers take eight extra sick days per year.[23] In a career of 30 years, this is 240 extra days. Considering that the average worker works about 222 days a year[24]—5 days a week, less vacation and holidays—smokers get paid for over a year that they do not work. New CDC figures assert that smokers cost the economy nearly $94 billion yearly in lost productivity.[25] On the days smokers miss, employers must hire untrained, temporary workers or see productivity decrease.

Smokers do not get as much done while at work. If they take a ten-minute smoke break every hour, then they miss nearly an hour and a half from every eight-hour shift. If they are denied smoke breaks, then their nervousness makes them more prone to mistakes and disputes with other workers.

Smokers lower morale in a workplace because other workers consider them lazy for taking so many breaks when others are still working.

Smokers are also more irritable, especially if they do not get to smoke as often as they want. Smokers have disproportionately higher rates of behaviors dangerous to themselves, others, and property. Smokers commit a disproportionate number of such acts as sexual harassment and other abuses directed against coworkers on the job.[26]

Employers with smokers on the payroll are forced to divert substantially higher amounts of funds for health insurance. This reduces the funding amount available for salaries and benefits for nonsmokers.

The Bible places emphasis on working and supporting one's family (Genesis 3:19). Paul said, "But if any provide not for his own, and specially for those of his own house, he hath denied the faith, and is worse than an infidel" (1 Timothy 5:8). God condemns laziness (Proverbs 6:6), requires that we treat others fairly (Matthew 7:12), and obliges us to give a full day's work for a full day's pay (Romans 12:17). Don't let smoking limit your options in getting a good job with a good salary.

Now that you know the negative consequences of smoking, why would you want to smoke? Are there really any benefits to lighting up? The only people who benefit from smoking are the people who sell cigarettes!

Discussion Questions

1. More than 6,000 people under age eighteen will smoke their first cigarette today. What influences so many teens to smoke?

2. List ways that smoking makes a person less attractive socially.

3. Why don't teens want to date a smoker?

4. Why do teens turn to smoking when they want attention?

5. Explain why experts call cigarettes a "gateway drug."

6. Describe the enjoyable effects of smoking. Describe the damage that smoking does to the body, even if you don't get cancer.

7. How does smoking affect athletic ability? Why don't successful athletes smoke?

8. Cigarettes have about 4,000 chemicals in them, including several poisons. How does taking poison into your body conflict with 1 Corinthians 6:19 and Romans 6:11–18?

9. Though smoking may temporarily ease stress, it will eventually lead to greater stress. Give examples of stress and problems created by smoking.

10. Employers don't like to hire smokers. List reasons that smokers are bad employees.

CHAPTER 6

THE PROS AND CONS OF STARTING THE SMOKING HABIT

Lesson text: Romans 12:1–2
Memory verse: "Let your light so shine before men, that they may see your good works, and glorify your Father which is in heaven" (Matthew 5:16).

An old Indian chief once told his braves that they ought to smoke. He gave them four reasons:

» Odors will repel bad dogs, mosquitoes, and skunks.

» Squaws will have to do all the work, for you braves will be short of breath.

» You won't have to worry about old age or confinement to the tepee or the reservation. If you smoke you will die before you get old.

» If you smoke, you'll save the expense of buying, keeping, and feeding a watchdog. You will be coughing all night, and prowlers will be frightened away, thinking you are awake.

Did you notice that third item? Smoking not only affects the quality of life, it often leads to an early death. Still, in our society, smoking has a certain appeal to many people. As Christians, young people face a serious choice when confronted with the temptation to smoke. Let's consider the pros and cons of smoking so you can make an educated choice about whether or not to begin this habit.

Smoking adds excitement, but it wastes your money

For some young people, it is exciting to get cigarettes and sneak away to smoke without being caught. There is a thrill that comes from doing something new, especially something forbidden. Solomon said, "Stolen waters are sweet, and bread eaten in secret is pleasant" (Proverbs 9:17; cf. Psalm 19:12; 90:8; Ecclesiastes 12:14). But such thrills come at a high cost (literally).

A few teens have parents who give them plenty of money to spend, but most don't. Their parents give them what they can spare, and they get a job to make a little spending money. Usually, the jobs teens can get don't pay much—especially after taking out taxes and paying for gas to go to work.

I just checked the corner convenience store and found a pack of Marlboros here costs $3.59.[1] Adding the 8 percent tax makes it $3.88. You might say, "Big deal. Four bucks." It really is a big deal, because if one's attitude toward money is so naïve, then he will never do well financially. Solomon said, "He becometh poor that dealeth with a slack hand: but the hand of the diligent maketh rich" (Proverbs 10:4). A lack of judgment makes many poor (Proverbs 13:23).

Think about those four dollars. The average smoker smokes 13 cigarettes a day,[2] 91 per week. There are 20 cigarettes in a pack, so that's 5 packs a week. Five packs costs $19.40 a week, $84 a month, and $1,008 a year. A thousand bucks a year is a lot of money to set on fire! If the habit grows to two packs a day (as it does for many teens,[3] especially boys), the cost jumps to almost $3,000 per year. Many teens are thinking about going to college, and coming up with the money is always an issue. The extra $4,000 gained by not smoking in high school will pay for the first semester at most colleges, and for the first year at some.

Some teens don't think much about the big picture of life after college (LAC), but if you've read this far, then you probably have more sense than the average youth. So think about this. If you begin smoking at age 14[4] (the average beginning age) and stop smoking at age 62 (the average age at which male smokers die, 13 years before nonsmokers), then you will spend $70,000 on cigarettes in your lifetime (a pack a day for 48 years). This is assuming that cigarettes are still $3.88 forty-eight years from now (we all know they'll be more).

Think of what you could do with $70,000! It would pay for some nice vacations. It would send your children to a good university. It would let you live in a nicer part of town. It would allow you to give generously to the Lord's work (1 Corinthians 16:2) or charity (Ephesians 4:28).

But that is only a part of the financial picture. In the book, *The Price of Smoking*, Duke health economists calculated that the real price over a lifetime of smoking is $40 a pack. They calculated this sum by analyzing all the costs of smoking—including expenses for cigarettes and excise taxes, for life and property insurance, medical care for the smoker and for the smoker's family, and lost earnings due to disability.[5] Their analysis found that the cost for a 24-year-old smoker over sixty years was $220,000 for a man and $106,000 for a woman.[6] Now, what could you do with a quarter million dollars?

There are also hidden financial losses not covered here. For instance, smokers lose money on the resale value of their cars and homes. They spend extra on dry cleaning and teeth cleaning. They typically earn less and receive less in pension and Social Security benefits, because they die sooner.[7] Truly, "He that loveth pleasure shall be a poor man: he that loveth wine and oil shall not be rich" (Proverbs 21:17). Don't let smoking make you poor.

Smoking may take off a few pounds, but it is not good for body shape and complexion

Some teens—especially girls—smoke to control their weight. Smokers, on the average, weigh seven pounds less than nonsmokers.[8] (Most people only gain five pounds when they quit, and five pounds is pretty easy to lose). There are two reasons for the lower weight in smokers. Smoking increases the body's metabolic rate—the rate at which calories are burned. Nicotine also acts as an appetite suppressant by lessening one's sense of taste and smell.[9]

But whatever benefits may be gained by weight loss are lost in skin and body shape. Smoking causes premature wrinkling and leathery, unappealing skin. Many are identifiable to strangers as smokers by their complexion, even when they are not smoking.

Many women spend considerable money and effort to try to maintain young-looking, wrinkle-free skin. Smoking accelerates the aging process by increasing production of an enzyme that breaks down collagen in the skin. Many smokers are as wrinkled as nonsmokers twenty years older. An 18-year-old smoker may have the skin of a 30-year-old. A 40-year-old often has as many facial wrinkles as a 60-year-old. The more one smokes, the greater the risk of premature wrinkling.

Although smokers tend to be thinner than nonsmokers, the effect of smoking on the endocrine system (glands which secrete hormones) causes smokers to store their body fat in an abnormal distribution. Smokers—women and men—are more likely to store fat around the waist and upper torso, rather than around the hips. This means smokers are more likely to have a higher waist-to-hip ratio (WHR) than nonsmokers. In addition to being less attractive, a high WHR (apple-shape) is associated with a much higher risk of developing breast cancer, diabetes, heart disease, high blood pressure, gallbladder problems, and cancer of the womb.[10]

Most of us want healthy bodies that are attractive to other people. God recognizes the body's importance, and in His Word we are instructed not to defile the body since it is the temple of the Spirit (1 Corinthians 6:19–20). God also acknowledges the role physical attractiveness plays in courtship (Genesis 6:2; 24:16; 26:7; 1 Samuel 16:12; Esther 1:11; 2:2, 7; Song 1:15), while warning against using the body as a sex object in dating relationships (Proverbs 7:10; Matthew 5:28; 1 Corinthians 6:18; 1 Timothy 2:9; cf. 1 Peter 3:3–4). Don't let smoking steal the beauty of your youth.

Smoking adds popularity but hinders social acceptability
There is a certain crowd that will admire you if you smoke. Smoking may open a door for you into a circle that once shunned you. Teens who smoke

often go to designated areas to light up. They congregate around the one that has the light, even when the weather is sub-zero. They are huddled up against each other, taking in the last drag before the break is over. It makes them feel connected.

Here is the real question: Is being in this group worth what I have to pay? Since a large majority of teens do not smoke (74 percent), being a non-smoker puts one in with the majority. Many of these are athletes and more popular students who have a strong opinion against smoking.

Few things put up a wall between people quicker than smoking a cigarette. Lighting up in public often brings immediate ostracizing and separation. People who know about secondhand smoke are strongly offended by smokers' disdain for others' health. Most teens don't like for their clothes to smell like smoke. Further, smoking during adolescence increases the likelihood of developing an anxiety disorder[11] which, of course, makes keeping friendships together an uphill battle.

I guess some people are good enough at making friends that this does not concern them, but many teens find fitting in a challenge. They discover that being accepted by others is difficult but very important.

The Bible speaks to both sides of this point. First, it instructs us not to follow a multitude to do evil (Exodus 23:2). "My son, if sinners entice thee, consent thou not . . . My son, walk not thou in the way with them; refrain thy foot from their path" (Proverbs 1:10–15). Don't feel like you need to please the wrong crowd. Don't let someone make you feel bad for not smoking.

Don't be down on yourself. You have strengths that others do not have. Think of your accomplishments in activities such as church, music, sports, or social clubs. Be an independent thinker. If you've got the guts to say no, then your life is going places. You have the right to an opinion as much as anyone else. You have the right to say no to smoking. Most people respect those who have conviction.

On the other hand, the Bible also speaks to us about the importance of the right kind of social acceptability. It tells us to avoid being unnecessarily offensive to others. "Let every one of us please his neighbour for his good to edification" (Romans 15:2). Paul said, "Even as I please all men in all things, not seeking mine own profit, but the profit of many, that they may be saved" (1 Corinthians 10:33). The early church had "favor with all the people" (Acts 2:47). This does not mean that we should compromise our convictions in order to please friends who want us to smoke, but it does mean that we can avoid offending the majority of people who are not in favor of smoking.

Smoking is a "rite of passage," but it displeases God

Because smoking is seen as a "grownup thing to do" (although 90 percent of smokers start as teens), some see taking up smoking as a rite of passage into adulthood. This may especially be true of teens whose parents smoke.

The real rite of passage into adulthood is becoming a Christian and living for God. This is where teens find the true fulfillment for which they are searching (John 10:10). Simply put, we were made by God for God (1 Peter 2:9). Serving God completes us.

God fully intends for our service to Him to begin sooner, rather than later, in our lives. The world's wisest king said, "Remember now thy Creator in the days of thy youth, while the evil days come not, nor the years draw nigh, when thou shalt say, I have no pleasure in them" (Ecclesiastes 12:1). Most people are mature enough to make a commitment to Christ by their early teens. Jesus was seeking after His Father's business at the age of twelve (Luke 2:42–49).

Now the question becomes, Does God care if I smoke? There is no verse in Scripture that says, "Thou shalt not smoke." Of course, the Bible is not primarily a "Thou shalt not" book. Its usual approach is to give guidelines and principles that help us make informed decisions. It does not, for instance, expressly say, "Thou shalt not take drugs" or "Thou shalt not molest children" or "Thou shalt not use Internet porn," but most people can discover God's will about these from Bible principles and examples.

So what Bible principles apply to tobacco use?

There is the principle of no self-inflicted wounds. Paul said we are to do our bodies no harm: "What? know ye not that your body is the temple of the Holy Ghost which is in you, which ye have of God, and ye are not your own? For ye are bought with a price: therefore glorify God in your body, and in your spirit, which are God's" (1 Corinthians 6:19–20).

Some teens say, "It's my body; I can do what I want to with it," but the truth is God owns everybody's body. If your friend borrowed your car or your iPod, you'd expect him to take care of it. If he brought it back to you wrecked or broken, you would make him replace it. He can tear up his stuff, but if he borrows yours, that is a different story. You see where this is going: We cannot damage the bodies God loaned us without upsetting Him.

Second, there is the principle of the Golden Rule. Jesus said, "Therefore all things whatsoever ye would that men should do to you, do ye even so to them: for this is the law and the prophets" (Matthew 7:12). Secondhand smoke does irreparable damage to families, friends, and strangers who happen to be near when one is smoking. We could say (some do): "That's tough. I don't care about others. If they don't want to smell it, let them go in another room or get another table." A Christian does not have this option. Paul commanded, "Let nothing be done through strife or vainglory; but in lowliness of mind let each esteem other better than themselves. Look not every man on his own things, but every man also on the things of others" (Philippians 2:3–4).

Third, there is the principle of the lighthouse. Every Christian's actions are to shine brightly as a positive influence for Christ. According to Paul, this is especially to be true of young people: "Let no man despise thy youth; but be thou an example of the believers, in word, in conversation, in charity, in spirit, in faith, in purity" (1 Timothy 4:12). Jesus commanded, "Let your light so shine before men, that they may see your good works, and glorify your Father which is in heaven" (Matthew 5:16). Even many non-Christians believe that smoking is a sin. Christian teens who choose to light up are putting their lights out with all these people.

Fourth, there is the principle of the body on the altar. "I beseech you therefore, brethren, by the mercies of God, that ye present your bodies a living sacrifice, holy, acceptable unto God, which is your reasonable service. And be not conformed to this world: but be ye transformed by the renewing of your mind, that ye may prove what is that good, and acceptable, and perfect, will of God" (Romans 12:1–2).

Can anyone say they believe it is the will of God that they smoke cigarettes?

Fifth, there is the principle of "don't give the reins away." We are not to give control of our bodies to anything but God's will. Paul said, "All things are lawful unto me, but all things are not expedient: all things are lawful for me, but I will not be brought under the power of any" (1 Corinthians 6:12).

Within eight seconds of a puff, nicotine arrives at the brain where it generates a flood of dopamine, resulting in an immediate "aaahhh" reward sensation. A 1–2 pack per day smoker takes 200 to 400 such hits daily for years. This constant intake of a fast-acting drug that affects mood, concentration, and performance, soon produces dependence.

Many teens know that smoking is addictive, but they vastly underestimate the addictive strength of nicotine. Experts classify nicotine addiction in the same category with heroin and cocaine. A leading expert on addiction, Jack Henningfield,[12] says nicotine is more addictive than heroin, alcohol, or cocaine. And tobacco also has a far higher death rate than heroin, alcohol, or cocaine.[13] One third to one half of occasional cigarette smokers graduate to physical dependence.

The University of Minnesota's Division of Periodontology found that tobacco is as addictive as heroin as a mood and behavior-altering agent. Nicotine is

» 1,000 times more potent than alcohol,

» 10–100 times more potent than barbiturates,

» 5–10 times more potent than cocaine or morphine.

But addictions don't happen to teenagers, right? Many teens mistakenly believe that one would have to smoke for years to become addicted. As few as two cigarettes a week can lead to addiction. Symptoms of addiction (strong desire to smoke, feeling tense when not smoking, being unable to stop smoking) can occur within weeks of starting to smoke.[14] Only 5 percent of teens think they will still be smoking in five years.[15] About 75 percent of them are still smoking more than five years later. Seventy percent of adolescent smokers wish they had never started smoking in the first place.[16]

It is actually easier to become addicted to nicotine as a teen than as an adult. When teens and adults smoke the same number of cigarettes a day, teens tend to become more dependent than adults. Those who start smoking young are more likely to have a long-term addiction.

How strong is the addiction? Although more than 80 percent of individuals who smoke express a desire to stop smoking and 35 percent try to stop each year, less than 5 percent are successful in unaided attempts to quit. Less than 10 percent of the nearly 20 million people who quit smoking for a day remain abstinent one year later. With only 2–3 percent of smokers succeeding in smoking cessation, cigarettes are considered among the most addictive drugs. Most tobacco-dependent persons never achieve lasting abstinence; half of them die prematurely of tobacco related disease.

There is only one sure way to guarantee that you will never become addicted to tobacco: don't pick up that first cigarette. Paul's admonition fits here: "Wherefore come out from among them, and be ye separate, saith the Lord, and touch not the unclean thing; and I will receive you . . . let us cleanse ourselves from all filthiness of the flesh and spirit, perfecting holiness in the fear of God" (2 Corinthians 6:17–7:1).

Discussion Questions

1. How would you answer this question: Does God care if I smoke?

2. How much does the average teen spend on cigarettes in a year? How much will it cost over a lifetime? Do you think God would approve of this use of money?

3. Do the majority of teens smoke? Does smoking make one more popular or less socially acceptable?

4. Apply this passage to the temptation to smoke: "My son, if sinners entice thee, consent thou not . . . My son, walk not thou in the way with them; refrain thy foot from their path" (Proverbs 1:10–15).

5. What is the true rite of passage into maturity for young people?

6. How would you answer a friend who wanted to smoke and defended it by saying, "There is no verse in the Bible that says, 'Thou shalt not smoke.'"?

7. What is the Bible principle of "no self-inflicted wounds?" (1 Corinthians 6:19–20).

8. How does the Golden Rule (Matthew 7:12) apply to the subject of smoking?

9. What is the principle of the lighthouse and how does it apply to smoking?

10. How addictive is nicotine compared to alcohol and other drugs?

11. Although only 5 percent of teens think they will still be smoking in five years, how many actually are?

12. What is the "body on the altar" argument against smoking? (Romans 12:1–2).

CHAPTER 7

HOLLYWOOD OR HOLY GOD? (A CHRISTIAN TV GUIDE)

Lesson text: 1 John 2:15-17

Memory verse: "Beware lest any man spoil you through philosophy and vain deceit, after the tradition of men, after the rudiments of the world, and not after Christ" (Colossians 2:8).

Hollywood is a district in Los Angeles, California, situated west-northwest of downtown. Due to its history of movie studios and stars, Hollywood is often used as a synonym for American film and television. It is the undisputed movie capital of the world, although much of the movie industry has now moved to Burbank and the Westside. Although Paramount Studies is the only major studio still physically located within Hollywood, in American culture "Hollywood" still stands for the entertainment industry in general. (The background history and information is adapted from Wikipedia.)

The influence of Hollywood on American culture is phenomenal. Although fewer than 200,000 people live in the Hollywood district, it exerts more influence than—arguably—any other single city in America. The income per capita in Hollywood is only $26,119, but it generates about nine billion dollars each year in movies alone ($23 billion if worldwide sales are counted). (http://news.ecoustics.com/bbs/messages/10381/207211.html.)

In early 1910, director D. W. Griffith was sent to the west coast to film in Los Angeles. His company visited the little village of Hollywood, and found that it enjoyed having the movie company filming there. Upon returning to New York, Griffith spread the reputation of this "wonderful place" called Hollywood. This caused other moviemakers to head west. The first feature film made in Hollywood, in 1914, was called *The Squaw Man,* directed by Cecil B. DeMille.

Though Hollywood is instantly recognized as the place where movies are made, music and television also claim a share of the Hollywood entertainment industry. Teenagers enjoy music, and many won't leave home without their iPods so they can listen to music constantly. In addition, most American homes have one or more televisions that often monopolize the family's leisure time. What kind of songs are teens hearing? What kind of television shows do they watch? Are we choosing Hollywood or Holy God?

Perhaps no other apple from the devil is as attractive and deceitful as the glamour of Hollywood. Movie stars seem to have it all—beauty, money, fame—and movies and TV shows wrap up life in delightful packages that make us sigh for romance, adventure, and happy endings. The worm in this apple is often hard to recognize. What guidelines should Christians use when consuming media?

Keep your ears clean

When we were children, it seemed our parents had an unusual interest in the cleanliness of our ears. (Why ears, as opposed to knees or toes, we never understood). God, our heavenly Father, seems to share that concern. Jesus often said, "He that hath ears to hear, let him hear" (Matthew 11:15), and He once criticized some for having stopped-up ears (Matthew 13:15).

In the 1950s, recording studios and offices began moving into

Hollywood. The famous Capitol Records building, with its unique circular design that looks like a stack of seven-inch vinyl records, was built in 1956. Unfortunately, much of what has come out of Hollywood's earphones is not fit for human consumption.

To have "clean ears," we must tune out ungodly lyrics, which serve as another form of bad advice (Psalm 1:1–3). The message of many teen songs is if you want to be in a dating relationship, "You have to give them what they want" (2 Timothy 2:22). Songs encourage listeners to be the "life of the party," but the message is, "Loosen up; one joint and a few beers never hurt anybody" (Romans 6:13). Job put the counsel of the wicked far from himself (Job 21:16). David prayed to be hidden "from the secret counsel of the wicked" (Psalm 64:2). On the other hand, Ahaziah "walked in the ways of the house of Ahab: for his mother was his counsellor to do wickedly" (2 Chronicles 22:3), as was Rebekah to Jacob (Genesis 27:6–13). Joseph of Arimathaea consented not "to the counsel and deed of them" (Luke 23:50–51), which is still the right course of action.

Have you ever had a song stuck in your head? You find yourself singing the songs you listen to frequently because they have become a part of your subconscious thoughts. Therefore we should be careful that the songs we choose for our playlist are the kind of thoughts that God wants us to have.

Keep your eyes focused on good things

Johannes Gutenberg revolutionized mass communications with the invention of the printing press. In the early 1800s, historian Alexis de Tocqueville remarked that newspapers had the extraordinary power to plant the same idea in ten thousand minds on the same day. That is dwarfed by the power of the single most influential invention in modern times (to this point even surpassing the computer)—television! Television can plant the same idea in hundreds of millions of minds in the same instant. And unlike the printed page, it does not require its viewers to be educated in the complex art of reading, nor does it ask them to form their own mental images and impressions. It delivers its messages with pictures and sound and all the enticements they can produce.

Since technology grew from the tiny, flickering screens of the 1920s to the surround sound, remote control, digital, 45-inch flat plasma screens of today, the marvels of television have become an integral part of American culture. Television entered the Hollywood scene in 1947 when KTLA, the first commercial television station west of the Mississippi River, began operating in Hollywood.

Television is a great tool for either good or for evil. Anything as powerful as TV needs some regulations. When dealing with Hollywood's choices from a Christian perspective, we need a "TV Guide."

A Christian watches TV realizing that God is watching him

We ought to be afraid to watch R-rated movies and suggestive TV because the Lord might return right in the middle and take us to the Judgment. There is an all-seeing eye watching us (Hebrews 4:13; 1 Peter 1:17–19; 1 Corinthians 6:19–20; Proverbs 4:26).

A Christian watches TV remembering that what is in his hand—the remote control—is one of the most dangerous things in his house (Ephesians 4:27; 6:10–13). Guns, knives, and poison can kill the body, but what comes through the TV can ruin one's eternal soul (Matthew 10:28).

TV involves more than innocent entertainment or killing a couple of hours. The devil is waging a battle daily for our hearts, minds, and souls (1 Peter 5:8), and television and music are two of his effective weapons. The musician Frank Zappa argued before a Maryland state senate subcommittee (when asked about some of his lyrics), "These are only words—words can't hurt anyone." He could not have been more wrong. Words, especially those set to music or put into actor's mouths, have outsized influence.

A Christian watches TV with his mind set in concrete

He has already made up his mind—sin is sin and wrong is wrong (Psalm 119:97–105). We ought to read the Bible before we watch TV, so our minds will already be "fixed" (Psalm 57:7). Our minds must already be made up about moral issues. The TV is not a reliable teacher when it comes to what is right and what is wrong. It sends mixed signals. Some things it portrays are exactly on target and beneficial to learn and live by. Other things in shows are against the will of God and dangerous to believe and follow. Most of us should watch much less TV than we do, and we should be careful to know what a show has in it before we submit to its teaching for an hour or two.

Those writing TV scripts are well-educated and effective. They know how to entertain an audience. However, some of them also have an agenda that they weave into their actor's lines. For example, many popular shows promote homosexuality as an acceptable lifestyle and portray anyone who has a different view as bigoted, intolerant, and hateful.

The writers effectively weave such themes into programs in subtle ways, and viewers may not consciously recognize the lessons they are learning. Enemies that come out in broad daylight brandishing a sword are much easier to conquer than ones that sneak in under cover of darkness. Physical persecution would be hard to bear, but at least we would know we were under attack. Satan attacks through media by eroding our character, spoiling our innocent pleasures, and cheapening our view of life. He does it so subtly that most are unaware of what is happening (2 Corinthians 11:3).

A Christian watches TV remembering that the devil usually writes the script

Professors S. Robert Lichter and Stanley Rothman interviewed 240 broadcasters and journalists from national media outlets such as *The New York Times*, *The Wall Street Journal*, *Time Magazine*, *Newsweek*, CBS, NBC, ABC, and PBS. They report that

- » Very few are regular churchgoers. Only 8 percent go to church or synagogue weekly, and 85 percent seldom or never attend. This compares to about 43 percent of the general population.

- » Ninety percent agree that a woman has the right to decide for herself whether to have an abortion; 79 percent agree strongly. This compares to about 50 percent of Americans.

- » Although most Americans believe homosexuality is wrong,

Lichter and Rothman found that 75 percent of the media elite believe it is okay. A mere 9 percent felt strongly that homosexuality is wrong. Again, this is far above the national averages.

» The majority—54 percent—do not regard adultery as wrong, with only 15 percent strongly agreeing that extramarital affairs are immoral.

Their conclusion? "Members of the media elite emerge as strong supporters of sexual freedom or permissiveness."

Should it surprise us, then, that the plots of many prime-time shows promote one or more of the offensive behaviors listed by Paul as keeping one out of the kingdom of heaven (Galatians 5:16, 19–21), when those who create the programs are not offended by them? Is it really any wonder that the perspective of news reporters tends to be favorable to homosexuals and abortionists? When we watch television, we must stop to think about who is teaching us (Proverbs 2:11; Psalm 32:8).

A Christian watches TV with his heart on his sleeve

He doesn't enjoy it when his values are attacked, mocked, or undermined by the comedian in the sitcom. One youth speaker said, "I never cease to be amazed at the number of students who come from 'good homes' and even attend private Christian schools who have watched one or more episodes of a teen soft-porn movie—typically, 60 percent of those whom I've surveyed." It is inconsistent to enjoy the very things which prompt God's anger. Paul wrote, "Who knowing the judgment of God, that they which commit such things are worthy of death, not only do the same, but have pleasure in them that do them" (Romans 1:32; cf. Colossians 3:1–6).

A Christian watches TV realizing that it has an off button that needs to be used

He would rather miss the end of an interesting program than watch some dirty part the producer threw in (Psalm 101:2–4; 19:14). Families should have rules about which programs are permitted and which ones are not. One parent complained, "My kid's all messed up from heavy metal music and exposure to sexual videos at an early age. You can't blame me for his problems. I'm never home!" That's much of the problem (cf. Titus 2:3–5). If your parents fall into this category, then be mature enough to set some thoughtful limits for yourself.

A Christian watches TV with one eye on his watch

Paul wrote, "See then that ye walk circumspectly, not as fools, but as wise, redeeming the time, because the days are evil" (Ephesians 5:15–16). TV is the biggest time waster in America. The average person would gain 47 hours a week (6.7 hours a day) simply by turning off the television! Most people watch television five times more than they read. In one year, the average American reads three books, 100 newspapers, 36 magazines, and 3,000 notices and forms, but he or she watches 2,463 hours of television.

» More than one out of ten Americans (13 percent) admit being addicted to television. (Some college students, for instance, schedule classes around a soap opera.)

» Forty-two percent admit watching too much television.

» Forty percent admit that watching television is not a good use of their time.

We might say we are not average and do not watch this much television. This may be the case, so let's say that we watch only half as much as the average teen. This still means that we could gain more than 23 hours a week by turning the television off.

Many teens say they do not have time to read the Bible every day, but when asked, "Do you have time to watch TV every day?" they inevitably say, "Well, of course." Most of us don't have to look any further than here to gain all the time we need. We would have time to read the Bible, pray, and visit the sick and shut-ins. Two rules might help us regulate our TV time:

» Don't turn on the TV until we have finished our Bible reading and prayer time.

» Turn off television one night a week and use that time for spiritual activities.

It takes self-discipline to break the TV habit, but Christian stewardship requires the effective management of our time (1 Corinthians 4:2). It is easy to come in, slide into a favorite chair, and hit the remote to "see what's on." Before we know it, one show has led to another, and we've wasted an entire evening. Pursuing any virtue requires mastery of the soul. Jesus said, "If any man will come after me, let him deny himself, and take up his cross, and follow me" (Matthew 16:24).

Hollywood is one of the great enemies of God's Cause in our generation. Of course not everything produced in Hollywood is bad, but many of its movies, songs, and television programs are unfit for Christian consumption. Unless we diligently monitor what we hear and watch, the line between worldly entertainment and Christian entertainment will blur and eventually disappear. If we as Christians condone the world's sins when they are disguised as entertainment, we will soon become like the world.

Keep this "TV Guide" handy. It might save a lot more than time.

Discussion Questions

1. When you think of Hollywood, what images come to mind? What are some of the good things that TV is used for? What major themes that contradict Bible teachings are often found in movies and television programs?

2. Analyze the time your family spends together. What do you do together? How long do you have together each day, counting weekends? What TV programs do you watch, and why do you choose those programs instead of others? Does your media consumption bring you closer together as a family?

3. What are the most popular songs right now? Are the titles and lyrics giving you good advice about making choices and living the Christian life? Why does it matter what songs say?

4. Pick a popular television show to discuss in class. Evaluate how the characters make choices about drugs, alcohol, sex, homosexuality, abortion, cheating on tests, and other moral issues. Even if they decide to do the right thing, think about how they come to that conclusion. Do they consult the Bible, a preacher/church leader, Christian friends, or parents, or do they just want to avoid getting into trouble? What value system do they follow?

5. Knowing that God is watching may stop us from listening to suggestive songs or watching immoral movies or programs. Why does God care about our entertainment choices? Consider John 3:16; Matthew 10:28; and 1 Peter 5:8. And remember the chorus to an old VBS song: "For the Father up above/Is looking down in love/So be careful, little eyes, what you see."

6. Are most TV writers and producers Christians? Do you think a writer/producer's views/values come out in their programs?

7. Have you ever said, "I don't have time to read the Bible, or _____ (some other spiritual thing)"? Is it wrong to waste time? Why or why not? Consider Ephesians 5:16. List some Christian activities the youth group could do if everyone spent less time watching TV.

8. Can you think of any TV programs or characters who sometimes make fun of Christian values? How does it make you feel to see Christ, the Bible, or those who are believers portrayed in this light?

9. If a friend mentioned to you that he felt he was watching too much TV, how would you advice him/her to change things? What steps would you take?

10. What are some ideas for alternatives to TV watching? What recreational choices might be better?

CHAPTER 8

DEALING WITH SEXUAL TEMPTATION

Lesson text: 2 Samuel 11–12
Memory verse: "Resist the devil, and he will flee from you" (James 4:7).

As we've discussed in Chapter 7, Hollywood doesn't just entertain; Hollywood glamorizes sin and presents enticing choices that conflict with morals and Christian principles. When Hollywood works with advertising and peer pressure, young people are bombarded with mixed messages, especially about sex. Society uses sex as a tool to sell products, to keep score and gain peer acceptance, to get and keep a boyfriend or girlfriend, and to entertain. On the other hand, parents, church leaders, and many medical, community, and academic leaders warn against the dangers and consequences of teen sexual activity; they encourage abstinence until marriage. No wonder teens are confused!

Where do we turn for definitive answers? Who can we trust to tell us the truth and help us make good decisions about sexual activity? First, consider the worldly view and contrast it with the biblical view.

PART 1: A BIBLICAL VIEW OF HUMAN SEXUALITY

Sex is not meant to be something that

- » is the only way to "prove your love" (Proverbs 1:10).
- » you feel pressured or forced into (Joshua 24:15).
- » you do because "everybody else is doing it" (Exodus 23:2).
- » you can't keep yourself from doing if you are in "love" with someone (1 Corinthians 9:27).
- » makes you feel used.

The Bible is a "light unto [our] path" (Psalm 119:105) and contains all we need to know in order to be spiritually complete and godly (2 Timothy 3:16–17; 2 Peter 1:3). So what is a biblical view of human sexuality? A biblical view of human sexuality includes specific definitions and principles to guide us.

God made us male and female

The physical differences between man and woman make it obvious that God intended for human relationships to include sex, at least for procreative purposes (Genesis 1:27–28).

God also intended for sex to be an enjoyable part of a married couple's life. Marriage was designed as a "one flesh" relationship, which includes the sexual relationship (Genesis 2:24). The wise man indicated that married couples were to find satisfaction, pleasure, and joy in each other's bodies (Proverbs 5:15–19; cf. Genesis 18:12). Paul taught that the sexual relationship is both a debt and privilege of marriage (1 Corinthians 7:1–5). The marriage bed is "undefiled" (Hebrews 13:4).

God never intended for sex to be a part of the dating relationship

Paul explained that lust was not God's will, commanding that each single person "abstain from fornication" and learn how to "possess his vessel in sanctification and honor" (1 Thessalonians 4:3–5; 1 Corinthians 6:16–19; Galatians 5:19–21; Colossians 3:5). God expects us to remain pure and holy throughout our lives. "For God hath not called us unto uncleanness, but unto holiness" (1 Thessalonians 4:7). While the marriage bed is undefiled, God will judge the sexually immoral God (Hebrews 13:4).

Why would God place such a restriction on the unmarried? Perhaps it is because of He wants us to be free—free of the problems that enter our lives through the door of promiscuity. Consider the following list of the freedoms found in sexual abstinence:

- » Freedom from the physical dangers of multiple-partner sex: sexually transmitted diseases, cancer of the cervix, and unwanted pregnancy.
- » Freedom from the problems of birth control: the pill and its side effects, the IUD and its risks.
- » Freedom from the pressure to marry too soon.
- » Freedom from the pain of giving your baby up for adoption.
- » Freedom from exploiting others or being exploited by others and all the emotions that result—guilt, doubt, worry, disappointment, anger, and rejection.
- » Freedom to be in control of your body.
- » Freedom to get to know your dating partner as a person.
- » Freedom to be in control of your life and your future—not to have it disrupted by pregnancy or disease.
- » Freedom to respect yourself.
- » Freedom to look forward to marriage and not be haunted by the "ghosts" of past sexual relationships.
- » Freedom to enjoy being a teenager, with many boy-girl relationships.
- » Freedom to form a strong marriage bond with one person for a lifetime—in other words, abstinence before marriage leads to greater trust, commitment, and faithfulness in marriage.

One's sexuality is under his or her control

A segment of society today says, "Young people can't control their desires. It is unreasonable to tell them to wait until they get married." God has more respect for young people than such shallow thinking shows. His Spirit inspired John to write of young men: "I have written unto you, young men, because ye are strong, and the word of God abideth in you, and ye have overcome the wicked one" (1 John 2:14). These young people were strong; they overcame the devil's temptations.

We do not discount the power of sexual temptation, especially in a sex-saturated society. But "greater is he that is in you, than he that is in the world" (1 John 4:4). If we resist the devil, he will flee from us (James 4:7). Strong faith overcomes the world (1 John 5:4). Here are two strategies to use to avoid falling:

» Avoid tempting places and relationships (1 Corinthians 15:33);

» Find the right kind of person and get married (1 Corinthians 7:9).

To avoid fornication, we must first respect God, and then we must respect ourselves. One of the reasons young people (especially girls) give in to sexual temptations is that they have low self-esteem and are looking for approval. A confused generation sees losing one's purity as a rite of passage, and degenerate dates see it as their due.

To avoid becoming another statistic, know your self-worth (Mark 12:31). You are valued so highly by your family that if your life was threatened they would spend every last penny to see you safe and in good health. You are valued by society. As you enter the workforce you will contribute more than a million dollars to our nation's economy over the next thirty to fifty years. Most important, you are valued by the God who made you, loves you, and gave His Son for you. You are a child of the King! Paul wrote, "Wherefore thou art no more a servant, but a son; and if a son, then an heir of God through Christ" (Galatians 4:7).

If you know your worth, then you won't give in to society's myths. For instance, 25 percent of men surveyed believe that rape is acceptable if the man pays for the date. If a man feels you "owe him something" in return for paying for a date, he is mistaken. If a man feels that way, then he should date a prostitute and not a decent girl. Your purity is worth more than a fifteen-dollar meal and a twelve-dollar movie ticket. Have confidence in your principles and predetermined choices about sexual activity. Let there be no misunderstanding by those you date regarding your intentions or desires, and no second guessing your decision to remain sexually pure. Pay your own way to retain your independence if necessary, and always carry a cell phone or taxi fare so you can call someone or get yourself home if you need to.

Fathers are to be the protectors of their daughters' purity and pleasure
(1 Corinthians 7:36-37). Trust your father's judgment and let him be your confidante in your dating relationships. Don't hide things from him; he is on your side. Bring the boys you date home and let him be around them.

ONE'S SEXUALITY IS NEVER TO BE USED AS A MEANS OF GAINING POPULARITY

Having a biblical view of sex will not likely make you the most popular person in school (cf. Galatians 1:10), but it will gain you some recognition in heaven (cf. Matthew 10:32). Robert Frost wrote in his poem "The Road Less Traveled,"

> *Two roads diverged in a wood, and I—*
> *I took the one less traveled by,*
> *And that has made all the difference.*

You may feel alone, but you are not. Christ is with you every step of the way (Matthew 28:20). Your parents are with you (Ephesians 6:4). Your church is with you (1 Timothy 3:15). Your true Christian friends are with you (1 Samuel 23:16). Even a segment of society is with you. For instance, former Miss America (2003) Erika Herald wrote,

> Ever since I can remember, I've had a commitment to abstinence. I was fortunate enough to have been raised by two loving parents who

encouraged me to set high standards, to value myself, and to save myself for marriage. But I grew up knowing that I was lucky and that not every young person had the love and support that I did.

I saw many of my peers use sex to try to find that love and acceptance. But instead of being able to fill that void, many of them became teen parents, contracted diseases, and had their hearts broken.

Erika is a Phi Beta Kappa graduate of the University of Illinois and was a member of *USA Today's* All-USA College Academic Team. This three-time member of the National Dean's List was accepted to Harvard Law School.

She discussed her platform on nationally broadcast programs, including *The O'Reilly Factor, Good Morning America,* and *CNN*. Erika promoted the benefits of abstinence from sex, drugs, and alcohol to thousands of students, parents, school officials, and community members. She even presented written testimony to the Congressional Record, chronicling her experiences as an abstinence educator.

In its proper place, sex is a gift from God. Out of that place, it's a tool of Satan. Wait . . . then enjoy.

PART II: LEARNING WHAT NOT TO DO FROM DAVID AND BATHSHEBA

There are times in life when a split second can make or break the balance of one's days. A decision made in the heat of the battle or the heat of the moment can forever change life's course. Our preparation for these moments makes the difference. If we have properly trained our minds and developed our characters, we will be able to make wise decisions and live without regrets (2 Corinthians 7:10).

David's moment of truth came in 2 Samuel 11. On that evening he went for a walk from which, in a sense, he never returned. He began the walk as the most respected saint on earth—king of God's people—a rich, popular, powerful, and happy man with several wives and many children. He ended it as an adulterer, murderer, liar, and hypocrite.

As was the custom, he walked along the palace roof in the cool of the day. From this vantage point, he saw a beautiful woman, Bathsheba, bathing herself. He lusted and sent for her to share his bed. When she later sent a note saying she was pregnant, he tried to hide his sin. His bad decisions blotched his great life.

From David's story, we learn several valuable lessons about how not to deal with sexual temptation.

David didn't turn his head when he should have

He saw a woman's exposed body. This was not an unusual occurrence for a man who had several wives, but this woman was not his wife. He could have done what he had likely done in similar situations many times before, which was simply turned his head and looked in another direction. He could have walked off that roof and gone back to his business or even spent some private time with one of his wives.

But he did not. He kept looking. And enjoying. And thinking. And desiring. The rest reads like a *National Enquirer* article.

How does this apply to people today? Teens live "on David's balcony." Everywhere they look, they see exposed women and men all the time. They cannot drive down the street, work in their yards, or go to school (or perhaps even to church) without seeing enough flesh to cause impure desires to surface.

Look around you right now. It is likely that you are within range of temptation at this very moment. If you are in a public place, and if you let your eyes wander, you likely could see tight jeans, short skirts, plunging necklines, and form-fitting tees and tops.

If you are near a computer or cell phone, you are only a few clicks from forbidden territory. In fact, innocent searches often show us more than we wanted to see, and pop-ups peddle porn, regardless of how diligent we are in trying to keep them out.

If you are in your home and the television is on, then you are within about three minutes of a commercial with a scantily clad woman ("sex sells," you know) or a character in a show speaking innuendoes and showing off her body, or worse—perhaps much worse.

What should we do? What lessons should we learn from King David?

First, turn your head! Jesus said, "Ye have heard that it was said by them of old time, Thou shalt not commit adultery: But I say unto you, That whosoever looketh on a woman to lust after her hath committed adultery with her already in his heart" (Matthew 5:27–28).

We must watch our watching. David "saw" (2 Samuel 11:2) before he "lay with her" (2 Samuel 11:4), which is the natural order. If we can avoid the first, then we will never get to the second. Remembering that God is watching helps us to watch our watching. He sees our efforts to turn our heads—and He knows when we don't (Proverbs 15:3; Psalm 139:1–12; Galatians 5:19–24; Ephesians 2:3; 2 Peter 2:14, 18; 1 John 2:26; 2 Timothy 2:22; Romans 1:27). He likes for us to pray, "Create in me a clean heart, O God" (Psalm 51:10).

Second, keep occupied in wholesome activities. When spring rolled around, it was time for kings to go to war, but this year the great warrior King David stayed home. "An idle mind is the devil's workshop," the old-timers told us. David would agree. If he had been in the battlefield, he would not have been on the palace roof. When are we most likely to be tempted—when we are occupied with a task or when we have an hour to kill? A moving target is harder for the devil to hit.

Bathsheba bathed where David could see her (2 Samuel 11:2-3)

The Bible does not indicate whether or not Bathsheba purposely washed in public view. At the least, she was careless about exposing herself. At the most, she knew of the king's walking habits and deliberately placed herself where he might see her and desire to have her in his harem. Perhaps the truth is somewhere between these two possibilities.

Christian teens must not dress immodestly or act sexually flirtatious. Many girls (some guys) display themselves in a calculated effort to seduce the opposite sex (Ephesians 4:19). "If you've got it, flaunt it," is their attitude. Those who deliberately dress to excite lust are as guilty as those who lust. Others are only naive or careless in their attire and actions. But the end result is the same. "What someone thinks is his/her problem" is not the attitude of a Christian. Jesus said, "Whoso shall offend one of these little ones which believe in me, it were better for him that a millstone were hanged about his neck, and that he were drowned in the depth of the sea" (Matthew 18:6).

The Bible shows remarkable insight into human personality when it specifically warns men of mental adultery (Matthew 5:28), and cautions women about dressing immodestly (1 Timothy 2:9). It is equally wrong for women to think lustfully and for men to dress immodestly, but the danger is greater in the way the Bible states it. Experts say (as if it were not common knowledge) that men are nine times more prone to be sexually aroused by what they see than women are. Let us err on the side of caution when we choose what we will wear to school, church, work, the ball game, on dates, or wherever we go. Let us dress to please God, not man.

Sex outside of marriage is a big deal (2 Samuel 11:4–5)

Most non-Christian teens are nonchalant about sexual activity. They try to act like it is no big deal to experiment with their boyfriends or girlfriends. They assume that everybody does it, so why make an issue of it?

The reason we should make a big deal out of waiting till marriage to have sex is that God makes a big deal out of sexual activity. Moses' seventh commandment says, "Thou shalt not commit adultery" (Exodus 20:14). It is repeated in the New Testament (Romans 13:9; James 2:11). Each of the Ten Commandments protected something of value. The seventh principle protected the home. Sex is a sin against God (2 Samuel 11:27), the other person (1 Corinthians 6:9), and one's own body (1 Corinthians 6:18). It also has other terrible consequences (2 Samuel 11:5).

Failing to deal properly with temptation starts one down a destructive path

One sin often leads to another (2 Samuel 11:6–27). To cover his sin, David tried to deceive Uriah (2 Samuel 11:6–11). This failed, so he got him drunk (2 Samuel 11:12–13; cf. Habakkuk 2:15). David finally stooped to plot the murder of his loyal subject (2 Samuel 11:14–25). He sent Uriah's death warrant by Uriah's own hand and involved Joab in his sin.

Could it happen today? Has a young man ever gone dancing, lusted after his date, given in to fornication, conceived a child, hated the child's mother for causing him such heartache, lied to his friends and family, and coerced her to kill the child by abortion?

It happens somewhere in America every week. Most teens face such issues in at least one serious relationship, and sometimes much more often. How many began flirting with a worldly person, only to end up with a broken heart and a damaged reputation?

Sin cannot be covered up or swept under the rug (Numbers 32:23; Galatians 6:7; Romans 6:23). Like malignant cancer, it is progressive (cf. Psalm 1:1). Sexual sin often still leads to the same sins David committed: lying, deception, hypocrisy, murder (abortion, suicide), and occasionally to other sins such as child abuse and physical violence.

We must not underestimate temptation's power or say, "It'll never happen to me." David was a man after God's own heart (Acts 13:22), and it happened to him. Do you suppose David thought it would happen to him? But then along came Bathsheba. If David was not strong enough to watch and still resist, let us take heed lest we fall (1 Corinthians 10:11–12; Romans 15:4). This shows just how quickly a man can fall into sin. In an unguarded moment, the power of sexual sin can ruin a life. Such temptation is no respecter of persons.

The stakes are high. Sin often comes with a high price tag. Few sex sinners ever repent and return to God (1 Corinthians 6:9–10; Revelation 21:8, 27; 22:15).

To escape the eternal heat, prepare for the heat of the moment.

P.S. Fornication is not the unpardonable sin, provided we forsake it (1 Corinthians 6:9–11). The woman at the well who was living in adultery was offered a drink of the water of life (John 4:5–26). A woman caught in adultery was told to sin no more, but Jesus offered her hope and a fresh start (John 8:3–11; Galatians 6:1; James 5:16; 1 John 1:9).

DISCUSSION QUESTIONS

1. What does the statement "Teens live on David's balcony" mean to you? How can we learn from David what to do and not do in such situations?

2. What does the Bible mean when it says each is to "possess his vessel in sanctification and honor"? (1 Thessalonians 4:3–5).

3. What is sex not meant to be that contrasts with how some teens view it today?

4. What are some of the freedoms that sexually pure teens have that sexually active teens do not have?

5. How do 1 John 2:14 and 1 Corinthians 10:13 apply to those who say they cannot wait until marriage? (See also 1 John 4:4; 5:4.)

6. One strategy we studied to use to avoid falling into sexual temptation is to avoid tempting places and relationships (1 Corinthians 15:33). Let's explore that idea in a real world. After collecting this information, seriously consider how God would want you to handle each in the future.

    a. The next time you watch your favorite television program, grab paper and pen and keep track of the number of sexual references that occur in the program and the commercials. Don't forget to count mini-skirts, halter tops, bathing suits, and other examples of near nudity, as well as suggestive language and dirty jokes. How does one decide which television shows are appropriate to watch? (Philippians 4:8).

    b. At school or work, take one day and count the number of dirty jokes or sexual comments you hear, and notice how many people around you are dressed in tight or skimpy clothing—but turn your head after you count! How do you keep a pure mind in such surroundings?

    c. Analyze commercials or ads that use sex to sell a product. Does the product really have anything to do with sex? Why do advertisers try to sell cars by showing beautiful, scantily dressed women standing next to them?

d. If you are in a dating relationship, count the number of times in a week that your boy/girlfriend turns the conversation in a sexual direction—either as a casual reference, joke, comment, or in tempting you to participate in some form of physical activity heading in that direction.

7. How does self-worth, self-confidence, and personal faith enter into one's ability to withstand temptation and remain pure in a culture that celebrates sexual sin?

8. How important is it to "turn our heads" when we see something we should not? What activities should we avoid to keep from leading ourselves into temptation? (cf. Matthew 6:13).

9. How important is it to not "bathe in public" so that we become a temptation to others? What activities/styles equal "Bathsheba's bath" for teens today? (1 Timothy 2:9).

10. In David's case, how did one sin lead to another? How does that happen today? What steps can you take to avoid sexual sin?

CHAPTER 9

SHOULD CHRISTIAN TEENS DANCE?

Lesson text: Matthew 14:6–12

Memory verse: "Now the works of the flesh are manifest, which are these; Adultery, fornication, uncleanness, lasciviousness" (Galatians 5:19).

In matters of sexual temptation, the devil often disguises the worm in the apple as an acceptable activity. Dancing is an example. Our society accepts dancing as an appropriate social activity for all ages, yet dancing is often the introduction to lust and fornication. Webster's Dictionary says dancing is a "series of rhythmic and patterned bodily movements usually performed to music." Sounds innocent, doesn't it? That's what Satan wants you to think.

What does the Bible say about it? *Dance* (including *danced*, *dances*, and *dancing*) is used twenty-seven times in Scripture. Six Old Testament (Hebrew) words are translated *dance*, which generally mean "to whirl, twist, move in a circle or spring about." Two New Testament (Greek) words are translated *dance*, meaning "rapid motion; to dance; a band of dancers and singers."

Reading the twenty-seven occurrences easily shows that the words are used in two ways. The first is to "jump up and down with joy" (as we might if our team scores the winning touchdown as time expires). For example, David danced before the ark when it was returned to Jerusalem (2 Samuel 6:14–16) and Miriam danced when Pharaoh was defeated (Exodus 15:20). Thus *dance* is often used as a synonym for happiness (Psalm 30:11; 149:3–4; 150:4). Most Bible references fall into this category.

Second, *dance* is used in the sense of men and women interacting together in what we associate with dancing at a club, party, or prom. Every time men danced with women in both Old and New Testaments, it was condemned. For example, while Moses was receiving the Ten Commandments, the people in the valley made a golden calf and danced around it (Exodus 32:7, 19, 25). Moses strongly condemned it.

PART I: WHAT THE BIBLE SAYS ABOUT DANCING

Dancing is dangerous because it causes lust (Matthew 5:8; 2 Timothy 2:22)

Herodias' daughter, Salome, was invited to Herod's birthday party to dance (Matthew 14:6; Mark 6:21–22). According to British Bible commentator William Barclay, she was sixteen or seventeen-years-old and "acted as a dancing girl." He further observes, "The dances which these girls danced were suggestive and immoral." According to William McGarvey, American Bible scholar and member of the church of Christ, "The dancing of the East was then, as now, voluptuous and indecent."

Salome danced "before them." Her seductive movements "pleased" Herod. This word translated "pleased" (*aresko*) carries the idea of "exciting emotion" and refers to being sexually excited. Herod then made a rash promise to give her anything she wanted, even up to half of his kingdom. She requested John the Baptist's head on a platter.

Most people easily see that what Salome did was sinful, leading to the sin of others. A follow-up question helps in our discussion of teen dancing:

What if Herod had danced with her? Would her dancing have been any less wrong? The answer clearly is no.

Even those non-Christians who see nothing wrong with dancing admit that its drawing power is sex appeal. The *Encyclopedia Britannica*, for instance, states, "To a certain extent all dancing is sexually stimulating." Texts on psychology agree that dancing is an expression of the sex instinct. Medical science identifies dancing as a sex stimulant. The modern form of dance is said to have started with South American prostitutes who were simulating the act of adultery as sexual foreplay. Louis Guyon, one-time proprietor of *Paradise*, a Chicago dance hall, said,

> In over thirty years in this business I have come to the strong conclusion that dancing is just the beginning of other evils. Sex being the one most often led to, and I believe that this is what makes dancing inviting . . . thousands of boys and girls dancing in this very way who do not realize they are doing anything out of the way, and whose fool parents look on complacently.

Paul Southern wrote that dancing "is like building a fire under a tea kettle and daring the water to boil." Each new style of dancing involves slightly different body movements, but they are all basically sexual in appeal. Hugging and swaying to music, bumping and grinding, or suggestively gyrating produce sexual desire in dancers' minds. Sandra Humphrey pointed out in her book *Don't Kiss Toads* that no healthy man will deny that it is sexually arousing to watch a girl swing her hips and breasts suggestively to music. Men are not made of stone (Gospel Advocate Company, October 2001, ISBN: 0892253347).

What would we think if we saw a brother dancing with his sister like that, or a mother dancing with her son like that? It would be unnatural and embarrassing. If it is doubted that sex appeal is the basis for dancing, try to split up normal (straight) boys and girls and have the boys dance together in one room and the girls in another. End of party!

Consider some research:

- » In one study, forty-four boys were asked what their feelings were toward the young ladies with whom they danced. Forty-one (93 percent) said they thought about sex.

- » An audience of 1,500 men was asked, "How many can dance and not have evil thoughts?" No hands were raised.

- » In another study, 80 percent of men admitted to having lustful thoughts while dancing.

- » The Roman Catholic confessional reveals that nineteen out of twenty of their girls who go wrong attribute it to dancing.

- » Christian Dior, famous Paris fashion designer, admitted in a newspaper interview: "For the first time I have done away with corsets even for dance dresses. I have often heard men complain that in dancing they could not feel a living form under women's corsets."

This is not the testimony of straight-laced preachers or old-fashioned grandparents. These are men and women of the world. Surely if some of the devil's followers can see the evil of dancing, it is not hard for spiritually minded teens to come to the same conclusion.

Dancing is dangerous because it often leads to sex (1 Corinthians 6:18)

Dancing started in a house of prostitution, and it never got too far from home. It was invented as a prelude to fornication, and has often led to that end ever since. Just as social drinking leads to drunkenness, dancing leads to fornication. Children's homes say that nine months after school proms, they have extra babies to care for. Robert R. Taylor, Jr., quoted Clara Jones, field worker for the North Dakota House of Mercy, as saying, "Seventy-five to 90 percent of those that slipped over the edge and slid into sex sin and entered unmarried motherhood at the North Dakota House of Mercy tell one story—the modern dance" (*Dangers Facing Young People*).

Dancing is dangerous because of the atmosphere in which it usually takes place (Matthew 7:16–17)

Dancing is often associated with other sins, including immodesty, drinking, and drugs. The music, immoral lyrics, dim lighting, and immodest attire of some who attend encourage levels of intimacy that lead to greater temptations. The music beats raise the pulse rate; more adrenaline and sex hormones are released into the blood stream, which creates excessive energy and stimulates sexual desire. The body movement adds to the arousal.

Does the Bible say anything about the atmosphere of dancing? It speaks of "revellings" (*comus*) and lists it as a work of the flesh (Galatians 5:21; 1 Peter 4:3; Romans 13:13 where it is translated "rioting"). Revellings are what we would call wild parties. Comus was the Greek god of feasting and partying. His sacred rights consisted in feasting and drunkenness, in impurity and obscenity of the worst kind.

Thus the Bible teaches it is wrong to even put oneself in the atmosphere of dancing. If one plans only to attend and not dance, what man can say that he definitely will not be tempted when he sees pretty girls dancing? What girl can say she will not be tempted to dance once she gets there? Can anyone picture Christ dancing with a woman, or even going to a dance? (cf. 1 Peter 2:21–22).

Someone says, "But school dances are monitored, well-lighted, and chaperoned." Yes, but schools cannot monitor what is done before couples enter, what goes on in their minds while they are there, and what they do after they leave. The fact that they need chaperones should tell us something about the atmosphere.

Dancing is dangerous because it is moving pornography

Lasciviousness is a work of the flesh which bars one from heaven (Galatians 5:19–21). The word Paul used is found nine times in the New Testament. It is translated six times as "lasciviousness" (Mark 7:22; 2 Corinthians 12:21; Galatians 5:19; Ephesians 4:19; 1 Peter 4:3; Jude 1:4), twice as "wantonness" (Romans 13:13; 2 Peter 2:18), and once as "filthy" (2 Peter 2:7). Thayer says this word means "filthy words, indecent bodily movements, unchaste handling of males and females." In more common language it means "conduct which excites lust." Dancing clearly fits this category. To say plainly what Paul stated, those who dance are not going to heaven.

It cannot be denied that dancing excites lust; therefore, it is nothing less than "moving pornography." Even if it were possible for one to keep his mind pure while dancing, he cannot guarantee that he is not causing his date to stumble. Jesus used a graphic illustration of how serious it is to cause another to sin: It would be better to drown (Matthew 18:6; cf. 2 Corinthians 11:3). He also said it would be better to pluck out an eye or cut off a hand or foot and go to heaven, than to be whole and be lost (Matthew 18:8–9). A paraphrase might say, "It is better to enter into heaven not having gone to the prom, than having gone, to be cast into hell fire." Heaven is worth it all!

PART II: "YOU'RE NOT GOING TO THE PROM?"

Let's face it. Today's young people are in a social pressure cooker. Teens are in the world but not of the world (1 John 2:15–17). They desire to fit in with the crowd, but they stand out as a light does in a dark room (Matthew 5:16). In a sin-sick society, they are indeed peculiar (Titus 2:14).

Among the many misplaced priorities of America's young people and the media targeting them is the hoopla surrounding the prom. Teen-oriented magazines begin at the first of the year to promote this "once in a lifetime" event. Untold time and money are spent on what is considered the crowning night of one's high school experience. How many times have Christian teens faced a bewildered friend who says, "You're not going to the prom? This is the biggest event of your senior year! Why aren't you going?"

To make it through the teen years faithfully, they need the strong backing of their parents, fellow Christians, elders, and preachers. They need Bible answers to today's questions (1 Peter 3:15). They need lines drawn and sin spelled out. They need to know what is right and what is wrong and why. Here is what you can tell someone who wants to know why aren't going to the prom.

"I don't want to be a part of sinful activities." When Christian teens understand the dangers and sins associated with dancing, they can patiently explain why they don't dance. If pressed to just attend and not dance, then they need to consider further reasons not to place themselves in a sinful environment.

The Bible says we can judge a tree by its fruit (Matthew 7:16). Statistically, some of the worst things that happen to teens happen prom night, graduation night, and homecoming night: pregnancy, drunk driving, car accidents, rape, and more. It is the sinful things associated with the prom that Christians should have no part of. Lust, immodest dress, vanity, pride, wasting money, getting drunk, and renting a hotel and having sex may make one feel older, but they do not make one an adult. Instead, such actions show spiritual immaturity.

For some, the prom is a rite of passage. It is seen as a turning point, a half step into adulthood, or a test of maturity and responsibility. The one activity most often associated with the prom is losing one's virginity, or if that has already happened, then enjoying sexual pleasures with one's prom date.

While the word *prom* is a shortened version of the word *promenade*, it might as well be a shortened version of *promiscuity*. A Google search of the words *prom* and *sex* resulted in over 1.4 million hits. Admittedly, not all of these were concerned with sexual activity as it relates to the prom, but most were, including the very first one. This link goes to teenadvice.com and its "Prom Central." Here one finds a long list of links to articles about the prom. Among these articles was one about "how to have sex on your prom night." Among the other links were numerous articles that promoted prom as the night to lose one's virginity.

This thing is "not done in a corner" (Acts 26:26). Any Christian parent who does not know these things remains oblivious only by turning a blind eye to the whole situation. Dancing is sometimes ignored because parents and church leaders don't want to "rock the boat." It should be rocked! Dancing is a problem. Teens need to know what is right and be warned against things that will keep them out of heaven (1 John 2:14; 1 Timothy 4:12; 1 Peter 2:11). We must be prepared to give an answer that pleases God (1 Peter 3:15).

Preachers need to preach about it (2 Timothy 4:2), elders need to guard the flock against it (Acts 20:28), parents need to warn about it (Ephesians 6:4), and young people need to stand against it (1 Corinthians 16:13).

An ungodly world puts tremendous pressure on God's teenagers to join with them in worldly recreation. While not wanting to sin, God's teenagers do want to enjoy these years. It is for this reason that sin needs to be defined and lines drawn so that they can know what is right and what is wrong.

"I don't want to go to the prom because I don't want to hurt my reputation." The young people in the churches of Christ give us great reason to rejoice. In most congregations, the teens stand out for their zeal, attendance, singing, and benevolent works. Many are standing for the truth, reading their Bibles, and trying to bring their friends to Christ. They really want to go to heaven. It is not easy, but they are ready to please the one who died for them. They fulfill Paul's words to young Timothy: "Let no man despise thy youth; but be thou an example of the believers, in word, in conversation, in charity, in spirit, in faith, in purity" (1 Timothy 4:12).

Why throw all that away for one night at a prom? A faithful Christian's influence can be powerful, although teens often do not realize until later that others are watching. This influence has led many to Christ (1 Peter 3:1–2). Peer pressure can be positive as well as negative (2 Corinthians 3:2). Worldly teens have it backward when they expect Christians to feel ashamed for not participating in what they should be ashamed of!

"I don't want to go to the prom because I don't want to give the church a bad name in the community." A sinning Christian damages the church's reputation (3 John 1:9–11). If a adult member of the church is seen drinking at a bar, then the reputation on the church is hurt. If a Christian teen is seen dancing at the prom, then others will think less of the bride of Christ.

We must set the best example that we can for Christ. Jesus said a lukewarm Christian makes Him sick (Revelation 3:15–16). When friends see one who claims to be a Christian involved in a lustful dance, they think, "He is not different from me," or "Her religion is a sham." If a friend sees a Christian at a dance one night, is he more or less likely to listen when that Christian tries to teach him the gospel the next day?

A dancing teen has his light under a bushel (Matthew 5:14–16). One of the most valuable things a Christian possesses is a good name (Proverbs 22:1; Romans 14:21; 1 Corinthians 8:13; 1 Thessalonians 5:22). A good reputation is worth far more than the temporary popularity that goes with compromise and the pleasure that goes with sin (cf. Proverbs 11:21; Ecclesiastes 2:9–11; Hebrews 11:24–26).

Dancing hinders interest in spiritual things (James 1:27; 1 John 2:15–16). An old preacher observed that a dancing toe and the praying knee do not belong on the same leg. The amount of enjoyment and participation in dancing is almost directly proportional to the lack of participation in Bible classes and spiritual activities. Things that choke out the Word from our lives must be removed (Luke 8:7, 14).

Alternatives welcome!

In some areas, thankfully, proms are losing popularity, as banquets are coming into vogue. In some schools, it is possible to go to a banquet that is held separate from a dance. Some churches have prom-alternative events so teens can get dressed up, enjoy some time with a date, and not have to be in a sinful environment. There is nothing wrong with dressing like an adult, wearing makeup, getting your nails and hair done, buying a dress or renting a tux, or even staying out past your normal curfew. Christian teens can have fun and make memories to last a lifetime without all the danger and sin of a worldly school prom.

Let's all live as though Christ died yesterday and is coming tomorrow!

Discussion Questions

1. The Bible uses the words *dance* and *dancing* in two ways. Explain how each way compares with dancing today.

2. Give two biblical examples of dancing that had sinful results.

3. The *Encyclopedia Britannica* states, "To a certain extent all dancing is sexually stimulating." Explain how this applies to the

people who are dancing and the people who are watching others dance.

4. Review the research statistics and comments about dancing made by people in the world. If even worldly people admit that dancing creates lustful thoughts, should a Christian want to attend dances?

5. While the Bible does not say, "Thou shalt not dance," it does condemn "revellings" (Galatians 5:21; 1 Peter 4:3). What does *revelling* mean, and what sins, besides dancing, are often included in this activity?

6. Define *lasciviousness*. Dancing has been described as "moving pornography." How do these two concepts fit into a discussion of dancing?

7. How does dancing or even attending a dance affect a Christian's influence for good? Can a Christian who goes to a prom and not dance be tempted to dance once he/she arrives?

8. What did Jesus teach about the seriousness of causing someone else to sin? (Matthew 18:6).

9. List worldly attitudes and expectations associated with attending the prom.

10. What good might result if Christian teens encouraged one another to attend prom alternatives in the place of attending proms and school dances?

CHAPTER 10

WHAT ABOUT SWIMMING?

Lesson text: 2 Samuel 11:1–5; Matthew 5:28
Memory verse: "In like manner also, that women adorn themselves in modest apparel" (1 Timothy 2:9).

Many Christian young people have never been asked to consider if public swimming is right or wrong. Their parents took them to the beach for vacation and dropped them by the city pool for recreation. They saved up money for a trip to Florida during spring break and another after graduation. If they thought about it at all, they just assumed that it was acceptable to God and Christians to put on a bathing suit and hit the beach.

It is fair to say that most Christian young people want to please God and would not intentionally violate His will. They don't mind straight-forward teaching, but they want evidence. They don't want to believe something just because Mom and Dad do or because their preacher said so. They want to be shown from Scripture what is right and wrong. Once this is done in a clear way, they are willing to do what God wants them to do. This material is given to such youth for careful consideration so each can "work out [his] own salvation with fear and trembling" (Philippians 2:12).

Once more, the devil hides a dangerous worm within an activity that society accepts without a second thought While the Bible never states, "Thou shalt not engage in public swimming," it does teach principles about modesty, influence, and temptation. These principles lead to the conclusion that public swimming is wrong.

Public swimming is immodest

"In like manner also, that women adorn themselves in modest apparel" (1 Timothy 2:9).

Nobody questions whether it is right or wrong to swim. The question is this: Is it right for a Christian to wear immodest swimwear around others of the opposite sex? Public swimming is sinful because of what people wear (or don't wear) while they are doing it. It is a sin to dress immodestly and to watch those who do. Sin separates one from God's favor now (Isaiah 59:1–2) and, eventually, will separate one from heaven (Revelation 21:27).

How can we determine what is modest? *Modest* (*kosmio*) can apply to a salary, house, or clothing. It is something moderate, appropriate, and humble. In 1 Timothy 2:9, it means "well-arranged . . . decent, modest" (*Vine's Expository Dictionary of New Testament Words*). English dictionaries define *modest* as, "decent or chaste; not calling attention to one's body" (Thorndike-Barnhart) and "behaving according to a standard of what is proper . . . especially not displaying one's body" (Webster).

We can be immodest, then, by wearing too much or too little. Wearing tuxedoes to Sunday worship, with diamonds and gold on each finger, would be immodest even if the body was fully covered. Modest apparel is clothing that does not draw attention to a person. It also de-emphasizes the sexual aspects of the body and thereby does not arouse evil desires in others.

How can we determine what is modest? Is it just left up to the individual or to societal norms? No, God's Word is our standard in all spiritual decisions (2 Peter 1:3). One helpful principle comes from Adam and Eve. They had covered themselves with fig leaves (similar to swim attire), yet God was not satisfied. He clothed them in animal skins (Genesis 3:21). The word used here (*ore*) indicates "a covering from the shoulder to the knee" (*Wilson's Old Testament Word Studies*), and gives insight into how much of the body God wants covered. No swimsuit comes close to covering from the shoulder to the knee.

Can anyone say with a straight face that today's swimsuits are modest? Men's trunks cover very little of the body and often give a shocking display of their anatomy. Women's suits leave almost nothing to the imagination. This is true whether a suit is a one-piece or a two-piece. Even the world admits they are too revealing. Commercials encourage girls to go "as bare as you dare." (You would need the guts of a burglar to wear what some wear to the beach these days.) A sports fitness club ad said, "It's that time of year again, when it's hard to tell a birthday suit from a bathing suit . . . so we need to get our bodies in shape."

A report in *The Dallas Morning News* revealed that 57 percent of men judged women's swimsuits to be "just about right." Amazingly, 33 percent said they were too revealing. Fifty-nine percent of women thought swimsuits were too revealing and 33 percent judged them to be "just about right." Could worldly people be more honest than some church members? Jesus once said, "The children of this world are in their generation wiser than the children of light" (Luke 16:8).

Some reason, "Sure, it would be wrong to wear a skimpy bikini, but a one-piece swimsuit is modest enough." Bikinis are worse than other swimsuits, but let's be honest; both are immodest. One-piece suits reveal all of the legs, most of the back, much of the shoulders and chest, and due to the skin-tight fit, leave very little of the private parts of the body to the imagination.

Lesser-of-two-evils-reasoning could justify many sins. One could say, "It is wrong to get passed-out-drunk, but it is not wrong to drink a few beers with my friends" (cf. Matthew 24:49); or "It would be wrong to use cocaine, but a marijuana joint wouldn't be that bad" (cf. Romans 6:13). This kind of thinking says, "It would be wrong to shoplift from Wal-Mart, but it is not wrong to claim a few extra deductions on my income tax" (cf. Ephesians 4:28).

Someone mused that wearing a swimsuit is like answering the doorbell in your underwear—except underwear probably covers more, and fewer people would see you. In Bible times, one was considered naked if his undergarments showed (see the American Standard Version footnote on John 21:7, where *gumnos*, naked, is used when undergarments were worn).

Some might say, "Since everybody at the beach is dressed that way, then there is nothing immodest about it. It is just accepted." Do circumstances determine modesty? Today's fashions may not seem all that bad to us because we have grown accustomed to them. Worse things than this were happening in Sodom, and people got used to them, too (Genesis 19), but that did not make homosexuality right.

Consider this reasoning in other contexts. Nobody at a bar thinks there is anything wrong with drinking, but that does not make it right (Proverbs 20:1; Proverbs 23:29–35; Ephesians 5:18). Nobody at a gay bathhouse thinks there is anything wrong with homosexuality, but that does not mean it pleases God (Romans 1:18–24). Everybody in the American Atheist Society denies that God exists, but this majority is wrong (Psalm 14:1). Sin is sin, and wrong is wrong, no matter how many people do it (Proverbs 11:21). "Everybody thinks it is okay" has never been a safe standard—from the flood (Genesis 6:1–7) until now.

Public swimming is a stumbling block to others

"But whoso shall offend one of these little ones which believe in me, it were better for him that a millstone were hanged about his neck, and that he were drowned in the depth of the sea" (Matthew 18:6).

Public swimming is sinful because it causes others to lust. Jesus said it would be better to drown than to cause another to stumble. The issue is much more serious than some take it. One day, "The Son of man shall send forth his angels, and they shall gather out of his kingdom all things that offend, and them which do iniquity" (Matthew 13:41; cf. Romans 14:15). In other words, if I am a stumbling block, He will not allow me into heaven.

Does anybody notice? Some might say, "Nobody pays any attention at the beach. Everybody wears swimsuits. They've all seen it before." This is simply self-delusion. To say that men don't notice women whose bodies are on display is to ignore basic biology. This is the very reason many go to the beach in the first place. *The Dallas News* report further reported that:

> Last June the Merit Report asked both men and women their reasons for going to the beach. More than 60 percent of men and women agree that men go mainly to watch. When it comes to why women go, the sexes differed. Men were apt to say women go to be watched (42 percent). Women reported they go to sun themselves more than anything (42 percent), although 30 percent said "to be watched."

Most people want to be noticed, and the quickest way to do this is to be undressed in the presence of the opposite sex. People do notice, and for the wrong reasons. An old preacher said, "The problem is, they desire to be chased, not chaste." Yet the Bible commands young women to be chaste (Titus 2:4–5), which means "innocent, modest, pure."

But someone might say, "Well, that might be true in the world, but Christians could swim together and not have problem since they have clean hearts." But this is simply not the case! Just because one has been baptized does not mean that he no longer has hormones and desires. The passages of Scripture that we are studying in this chapter were addressed to Christians (1 Timothy 2:9; 1 Peter 2:11). Consider what one Christian young man confessed:

> I started thinking about my teenage years, when I would sit up in the condo room with binoculars looking at women walking on the beach. Surprisingly, I never found anything wrong with that—even though I was a Christian at the time. I didn't exhibit this type of behavior at home, but when I was at the beach, there was something different about watching the women—to be honest, it was what they were wearing (or not wearing).
>
> I liked walking on the beach with mirrored sunglasses so I could "check out a girl" without her noticing. I wasn't the only one—all my male friends were "noticing the girls," too.

Yes, noticing girls is natural, but not the way we were looking at them. We were not thinking about how beautiful their faces looked; in fact, we couldn't have picked them out of a line-up later if they had been properly clothed.

When my friends had pool parties, we always wanted to invite the girls we wanted to see in bathing suits. If you don't believe me, visit a guy's locker room and listen to what "normal guys" say. Men who say they are not tempted to lust after women in immodest clothes are gay, sterile, or lying. That is just the way God created us. In a marriage relationship this is pure and natural, but outside of marriage it is wrong (Matthew 5:28; Galatians 5:19; 1 John 2:16).

Cliff Lyons wrote an article entitled "Immodest Dress—Who's Watching?" In it he talked about an elder who said, "I used to have swimming parties at my house, but I stopped when I took time to observe how the men were looking at the women. I wanted no part in this." The article told of another Christian who said, "Until a few years ago I simply was not convinced there could be anything wrong with public swimming."

What changed his mind? He and his wife went with another couple to the lake. When he saw his friend's wife in her bathing suit, he found himself having impure thoughts that he had never had when she was properly clothed. He spent the rest of the afternoon with his back turned to her to avoid evil thoughts. He said he told himself over and over, "This is what preachers have been trying to tell me, and I didn't believe them" (*Glad Tidings of Good Things*, 2.23.98, Jacksonville church of Christ, Jacksonville, Alabama).

Who is to blame when one lusts after another? The one who lusts is without excuse, no matter what others are wearing, but those who dress in a provocative manner are not innocent either. The darkest chapter in King David's life began by looking on Bathsheba in her "bathing suit" (2 Samuel 11:1–5). Her initial sin was a thing thought of today as quite harmless—she was immodestly clothed. No big deal. So she showed a little skin. It wasn't anything David hadn't seen before. Besides, those were modern times. You know, modern age, modern morals. So what if the neighbors got an eyeful once in a while. It wasn't her fault. They shouldn't be looking.

David should have turned his head, but Bathsheba should have been more careful about where she bathed. What woman would dare accuse David of just being dirty-minded? What man would say that he is stronger than "a man after God's own heart"? (1 Samuel 13:14; Acts 13:22). If David could be tempted, then any man can. We are responsible if we cause a brother to stumble (1 Corinthians 8:13).

Another interesting case in point also comes from the Old Testament. God's priests in those days wore robes instead of pants. God forbade them to build high altars that required steps, lest those below see their nakedness (Exodus 20:26). They could have reasoned, "They should not be trying to look up our robes! We're just trying to offer a sacrifice."

God later told them to make linen breeches (*miknac*, "hiding; garment for concealing the private parts") to wear under their robes (Exodus 28:40–42), to cover them when they were in such a position. It is interesting that God used the same standard of modesty here as He did in Genesis 3 and the same standard for men as for women. The priest's garments were to cover "from the loins even unto the thighs" (Exodus 28:42). Since the thigh reaches to the knee, a conscientious person finds tucked away in God's Word another clue to modesty.

Just as they had to be careful under all circumstances to keep themselves covered, God's priests today, Christians (1 Peter 2:9; Revelation 1:6), must be careful not to expose too much under any circumstances—even in their recreation and vacation time (and even if no one knows them).

The power of visual stimuli. The Bible draws a clear connection between visual observation and lust. Advertisers are aware of the value of a sexual stimulus, as shown in the constant display of flesh in television and magazine commercials.

Biologically and psychologically, men and women differ. While there are exceptions, men are usually more sexually aggressive than women (men's sexual desires are said to be six to ten times stronger than women's). Men are much more likely to be visually stimulated (excited by what they see) than women, who are more likely to be environmentally (relationship) stimulated. It is no accident then that Paul, in 1 Timothy 2:9, directed the instruction on modesty primarily to women and that Jesus warned men about looking at women (Matthew 5:28). The Bible could have reversed the genders, but the God who made us, knows us (John 2:25).

In practical terms, this means that clothes that might not seem too revealing from a woman's point of view may be seen differently by men. Women should take this into consideration when choosing what to wear (Romans 14:13). Young women must be taught the power they exercise over men, simply by sight and touch (cf. Proverbs 7:10, 21–22), and the responsibilities that this brings upon them.

Human attraction is powerful. Most adolescent males have a difficult time with the frustrating sexual stirrings they are experiencing. The temptation of seeing girls with little clothing on makes controlling these feelings in a God-honoring way much harder. In our permissive society, many husbands also find it challenging to stay faithful to their marriage vows, especially with the temptation immodesty brings.

While women and girls could take a "that's his problem" attitude, this would be inconsistent with the attitude of Christ found in Philippians 2:1–5. It is easier for women to wear modest clothes than for men to pluck out their eyes (cf. Mark 9:43–49). On the other hand, it should also be said that men should recognize that what is "good for the goose is good for the gander" and refrain from exposing themselves to the opposite sex. Both sexes must also make a "covenant with [their] eyes" (Job 31:1) not to look, regardless of what others wear.

Lasciviousness will keep one out of heaven. Immodest apparel is lascivious—a word we don't use much, but which means "something that causes lust" (from *aselgeia*, "filthy words, indecent bodily movements, unchaste handling of males and females; unbridled lust; shamelessness"). Whatever tends to excite lust, either in ourselves or in others, is lascivious (Galatians 5:19; cf. Mark 7:22; 2 Corinthians 12:21; Ephesians 4:19; 1 Peter 4:3; Jude 1:4). Swimwear (as well as much sport and leisure attire) is purposefully designed to be lascivious. In many cases, it is even advertised as "hot," meaning "sexually attractive." To wear lascivious clothing is to become a part of the group that "shall not inherit the kingdom of God" (Galatians 5:21).

Public swimming is wrong because it puts one in a place of temptation

"Neither give place to the devil" (Ephesians 4:27)

Even if we went to the public beach fully clothed, it would be sinful because it unnecessarily places us in the way of temptation. We could not honestly pray, "Lead us not into temptation" (Matthew 6:13) and then lead ourselves into it. Paul said, "Neither be partaker of other men's sins" (1 Timothy 5:22).

Someone might say, "People dress immodestly everywhere you go." It is true that we can never get completely away from immodest dress. We see it at the grocery store, post office, and, even in church services. However, there are certain places and activities known for immodesty, such as a pool party, crowded beach, or water park. One can see alcohol at the grocery store, but that does not make it right to go to a bar to drink a soft drink. The same thing is true with television shows: there are some that are known for inappropriate material and should be avoided. We should be wise enough to stay away from places where our souls will be vexed with temptation and susceptible to sin (cf. 2 Peter 2:7).

We must be "sober" (watchful) lest Satan devour us (1 Peter 5:8). Avoiding his grip is challenging enough without purposely placing ourselves into one of his most effective traps (cf. 2 Timothy 2:26). James says, "Resist the devil and he will flee from you" (James 4:7). He did not say "assist" the devil. Paul commanded us not to "give place to the devil" (Ephesians 4:27), which means give him any advantage in tempting us. Any normal man is tempted to think unholy thoughts when in the presence of scantily clad women at a pool or the beach (cf. 1 Peter 2:11). Women can also be tempted by seeing men's unclothed bodies. Why should Christian teens put themselves in the way of sin, which is the way of death? (cf. James 1:14–15).

God's teens are to be pure in mind (2 Peter 3:1), conscience (1 Timothy 3:9), language (James 3:2), and body (Hebrews 10:22). We must "eschew evil" (1 Peter 3:11)—want no part of it—and "have no fellowship with the unfruitful works of darkness" (Ephesians 5:11). We can become a partaker of another's evil deeds (2 John 1:10–11; cf. Romans 1:32). Public swimming violates each of these principles.

Some men think they can let evil thoughts roam free in the pastures of their minds—as long as they do not act on them. The Lord condemns lust. He said, "Whosoever looketh on a woman to lust after her hath committed adultery with her already in his heart" (Matthew 5:28). The man who lusts after a woman has sinned—whether or not he says or does anything further. The Lord expects us to stay clean, even in thought (Proverbs 4:23; Philippians 4:8). And the thought leads to deed, given opportunity (James 1:13–16). With this is mind, why go where we know we will be tempted, and thus decrease our chances of going to heaven?

Public swimming is wrong because it can indicate a hardened heart

". . . with shamefacedness and sobriety" (1 Timothy 2:9).

God wants His children to be sober and shamefaced. These are not terms we use very often so let's define them. *Sobriety* (*sophrosune*) denotes "soundness of mind; self-control; good judgment, moderation . . . especially as a feminine virtue, decency." Vine says that *shamefacedness* indicates "a sense of shame, modesty." The American Standard Version uses the word *shamefastness*. Davies says, "Shamefastness is modesty which is 'fast' or rooted in character" (*Bible English*). *Fast* means "firmly fixed" as a "bedfast" person—someone who cannot get out of bed. A shamefast person is firmly fixed in a sense of shame or modesty. Shamefacedness is the opposite of boldness or brazenness. This word indicates the ability to blush.

Wearing a swimsuit in public should cause us to blush; if it does not, we should examine our hearts to see if they are "seared with a hot iron" (1 Timothy 4:2). Modest teens retain the ability to blush if someone sees too much of them. Most worldly people consider this an undesirable trait, but God likes it. Some of Jeremiah's neighbors' blushing mechanisms had malfunctioned: "Were they ashamed when they had committed abomination? nay, they were not at all ashamed, neither could they blush: therefore they shall fall among them that fall" (Jeremiah 6:15; cf. 3:3; 8:12).

Each Christian is a walking billboard. We advertise our hearts by our words, deeds, and actions. Modest clothes indicate a spiritually healthy heart. Immodest clothes indicate heart trouble. We are to "abstain from all appearance of evil" (1 Thessalonians 5:22), and we must look at our actions in light of the influence they have on others (Matthew 5:13–16). If we are modest and dress in a way that glorifies God, then others will respect the church. If we do not, we bring shame on Christ and His church. It is possible to "crucify . . . the Son of God afresh, and put him to an open shame" (Hebrews 6:6). None of us wants to do this.

So what about public swimming? As long as we are out of the view of the opposite sex it is permissible. It is also permissible if both sexes swim together provided all are dressed modestly. At the same time, the above Bible verses cannot be obeyed while wearing swimsuits in public places. If a swimsuit is acceptable in light of 1 Timothy 2:9 then no attire would be unacceptable.

If you refrain from swimming publically, your friends may not understand. Some people are going to "think it strange that ye run not with them to the same excess of riot" (1 Peter 4:4). However, Christians (saints—by definition different from the world) know they are "set apart" from the world (Romans 12:1–2; 1 Corinthians 6:17–18; Titus 2:14). Since we are called to holiness (1 Peter 1:15–16), we should stay away from things that may cause us to fall, even if we have done them all our lives (1 Peter 4:1–3).

Let's all study, consider, pray, and live so we will be judged faithful at the end. May all Christians live "soberly, righteously, and godly in this present world" (Titus 2:12).

Discussion Questions

1. Define *modest* as it applies to clothing. Is it possible to be fully clothed and still be immodest?

2. According to Scripture, how much of the body should be covered to be modest? In view of this, are swimsuits modest?

3. Some say, "Since everybody at the beach is dressed in swimwear, nobody notices." Is that true? Why or why not?

4. Do circumstances determine modesty? Is a sinful action no longer sinful because the people involved do not think it is wrong? (Who determines what is sin, God or man?)

5. Why is immodesty wrong? Give a Bible example of problems that developed because of immodest clothing.

6. Define the words *lust* and *lascivious*. How do these words apply to swimwear and public swimming?

7. Apply Ephesians 4:27 and 1 Peter 5:8 to temptations that occur when people go to the beach or a public swimming pool.

8. Have you ever been embarrassed by the immodest clothing a friend was wearing? Consider how Jeremiah 6:15 applies to public swimming and immodest clothing in general.

9. "Each Christian is a walking billboard." What effect does a Christian have on his or her friends when he or she dresses immodestly or swims publicly? Does it have any effect on how the church is viewed in the community?

10. What conditions should control whether a Christian can go swimming?

CHAPTER 11

HOW TO PROTECT YOURSELF FROM DATE RAPE

Lesson text: Proverbs 22:3
Memory verse: "Flee fornication" (1 Corinthians 6:18).

Victims of sexual assault are not at fault. Men who force women to have sex bear the full brunt of the guilt. Period.
    Victims of rape often harmfully ask themselves what they did to bring on the attack, or they feel guilty because they could not stop it. All of us need to understand that the victim did not cause the attack; in addition, she cannot completely defend herself against a bigger, stronger rapist. We lock our houses and install alarm systems, but if someone wants our property, he will find a way to break in, despite our precautions. And if a man intends to rape a woman, he will probably succeed, no matter how hard she fights. If you have been sexually assaulted, we support you. We encourage you. We pray for you. We are sorry that you had this terrible experience, and we want you to know that it is not your fault.

Date rape is especially terrifying because the victim usually trusts the man she is dating. She doesn't realize until too late that he is not a "nice guy." A man who would commit a date rape is given over to sin and selfishness, though he may seem charming and fun. Such a man has no qualms about practicing deceit—Satan's favorite tool!

If you are currently dating, please understand that though defense against rape is difficult, you can take some precautions to make you less vulnerable to attack.

How can you protect yourself from date rape?

» Date those who share your views on sexuality (1 Corinthians 15:33; 2 Corinthians 6:14).

» Don't be naïve—one who asks you for a date may not respect you as he should. You should not assume that he has the same moral values. Some who may ask you out serve "divers lusts and pleasures" (Titus 3:3) and walk "after their own lusts" (Jude 1:16). Some pretend to love their dates but really are only "lovers of their own selves" (2 Timothy 3:2). A servant of Jesus Christ has a different perspective from one in the world (Colossians 4:12). What views are prevailing?

» According to one survey, 50 percent of high school boys and 42 percent of girls said there were times it was acceptable for a male to hold a female down and physically force her.[1]

» In another survey, 33 percent of males surveyed said they would commit rape if they definitely could escape detection.[2]

» Twenty-five percent of men surveyed believed that rape was acceptable if the woman asks the man out.[3]

If you date those who don't share your views, then you may find yourself in a situation where your date is expecting sex after a couple dates, and he becomes frustrated, angry, and violent if you do not provide it. Date rape can be coerced, both physically and emotionally. Some emotional tactics include:

- » Threats to your reputation ("I'll tell everyone you are gay").
- » Threats to break off the relationship.
- » Name calling.
- » Saying you "brought it on" or "really want it."
- » Threats to say you did it even if you didn't.

Threats are nothing but extortion, which both civil law and the Bible condemn (Matthew 23:25; Luke 18:11; 1 Corinthians 5:10–11; 6:10). If someone makes such a threat, tell him your mind is made up, and if he wants to break up, then so be it. You are better off keeping your purity and your soul. A date who threatens you or tries to force you to have sex is not practicing Christian values; find someone else to date.

There is nothing you can do to stop the person from lying about you, but you can tell the truth, and your reputation will not be hurt as much by his lie as by your actual sin of fornication. Even if you give in and he does not tell his friends (which is unlikely), the chances are that you will one day break up; then he is likely to brag to others about his "conquest."

Keep a good reputation
This one may sound strange, but girls who have a reputation of sleeping around are more likely to be raped by their dates. Prevailing views are in many cases completely false, but the reality is that many men believe them and act based on these assumptions.

What are some prevailing views?

She's slept with other people, so she should sleep with me. Nearly 15 percent of respondents thought a woman would be partly responsible for being raped if she was known to have many sexual partners, and 8 percent believe that she would be totally responsible.

We've had sex before, and she didn't say no then. Do not allow yourself to be subject to peer pressure or encouraged to do something that you don't want to do. Solomon said, "If sinners entice thee, consent thou not" (Proverbs 1:10). "Blessed is the man that walketh not in the counsel of the ungodly, nor standeth in the way of sinners, nor sitteth in the seat of the scornful" (Psalm 1:1). You do not owe sexual favors to any man for any reason—except your husband, and then only after you are married (1 Corinthians 7:1–5). The only debt you owe is to God for saving your soul (cf. Romans 1:14).

We must be careful with our reputations and not let our speech, clothes, or actions contradict our beliefs. Solomon wrote, "Dead flies cause the ointment of the apothecary to send forth a stinking savour: so doth a little folly him that is in reputation for wisdom and honour" (Ecclesiastes 10:1).

Be clear about the kind of relationship you want

Let's face it: The majority of non-Christians assumes that a serious dating relationship includes sex, and many go into a casual date hoping (even expecting) to "score."

A Christian's good reputation will help to some degree (Philippians 2:29), but one cannot rely on reputation alone. You must speak up about your moral stance. The psalmist said, "Let the redeemed of the Lord say so" (Psalm 107:2). In other words, "Speak up. Be heard. Take a stand." Don't rely on hints and nervous jokes to get your message across. Don't assume your date will automatically know how you feel, or will eventually "get the message" without your telling him.

Joseph of Arimathea tried to be a secret disciple, for fear of what others might think or do (John 19:38). Peter tried to hide his relationship with the Lord. Neither was wise to do so. Peter ended up denying his Friend (Mark 14:68–71). Be bold and let your dates know where you stand (Acts 4:13). It will help to lower expectations and frustration. It will also take much of the pressure off the relationship and allow both of you to focus on what dating is supposed to be about: getting to know one another and enjoying social companionship.

One researcher suggested making the following statement to the one who has asked you out: "John, I am looking forward to our date. However, I want to tell you in advance, I'm saving myself for marriage. I don't want to have sex."

Or, "John, I am looking forward to our date. I thought I should tell you in advance that I never have sex because I wish to remain a virgin until I marry. I still want to go out, but if you have changed your mind, I will understand."

Or, "John, I am looking forward to our date. I thought I should tell you this in advance so there is no misunderstanding. I am totally opposed to sex until marriage. If you are the nice guy I think you are, everything I just told you has no relevance. I hope that I have not scared you away from me, because I am looking forward to our date and hope you still want to go out."[6]

A girl cannot risk dating someone even a few times before bringing the subject up. Forty-seven percent of rapes were on first or casual dates.[7] It may seem awkward, but feeling awkward is better than being raped.

Avoid compromising situations

Don't be alone with your date or any person of the opposite sex in a secluded place. College girls are warned that most rapes take place in the students' living quarters. Off campus victimizations can take place in bars, dance clubs, and secluded work settings. Do not go to his dorm room, your apartment, a parent's house when no one else is there, or a quiet room at a party. Since 71 percent of rapes are planned, go in a group with new dates. Some estimate that 88 percent of date rapes happen on the way home, so don't accept a ride in a car with someone you don't know well or someone you don't trust completely.

It has become common in our lax society for teen girls to be alone at home with their boyfriends, while the parents are at work or away at a restaurant. Some college couples go to each other's apartments or dorm rooms to watch movies or do homework. This is a recipe for one of two things to happen:

» Consensual sex (fornication);

» Non-consensual sex (rape).

Skeptical? Consider that the majority of rapes occur in living quarters—60 percent in the victim's residence, 10 percent in a fraternity, 31 percent in other living quarters. In one report, 25 percent of men surveyed believed that rape was acceptable if the woman goes back to the man's room after the date.[8] "Jennifer" posted "How to Protect Yourself from Rape" on the Web: "I was raped when I was 15, and I can only suggest that you never be alone with anyone that you don't know well enough, and never invite them over or go over there. Please understand that the results are very difficult to live with when you've been raped."[9]

Don't spend time alone with someone who makes you feel uneasy or uncomfortable

Does your "radar" go off when this person is looking at you? Does your mother's new boyfriend stare at you in a way that makes you feel uncomfortable? Does your boss or coworker touch you inappropriately, want to hug often, or make sexual remarks? Does an uncle or cousin give you "the creeps"?

Trust your instincts. Avoid this person as much as possible. Explain your concerns to your coworker, father, or mother, and ask them not to leave you alone with this person. Perhaps you are wrong, and if so, then no long-term harm is done. But if you are right, then you may have avoided unspeakable harm and heartache. Perhaps Jesus' words fit here: "Behold, I send you forth as sheep in the midst of wolves: be ye therefore wise as serpents, and harmless as doves" (Matthew 10:16).

Don't send the wrong message with your clothes (1 Timothy 2:9; Matthew 5:28)

Men, get this point first. Under no circumstances is rape ever justified. Regardless of how little she is wearing, or how flirty she may have been, no means no. There is no license to commit rape, and her clothing is not an invitation. If a woman were completely undressed and dancing provocatively, you still do not have the right to lay a finger on her.

With that said, ladies, we are talking about a real world, not a Christian one. We are not living in *Little House on the Prairie* days when most men where honorable and society quickly and severely dealt with a man who acted ungentlemanly toward a woman. These are the days of Howard Stern and Vegas strip shows. Society hardly blinks an eye at what would have been front page news in our grandparents' day. Minds are in the gutter, mouths are in the sewer, and the law's slap on the wrist is not a big deterrent to someone who wants more than a date is willing to give.

If you are interested in protecting yourself, you cannot ignore the fact that improper clothing can bring undesirable attention. For instance, years ago a Portuguese ship, the Santa Maria, was hijacked by rebel pirates. The drama was followed closely by the news media. According to newspaper accounts, one of the first things that happened on board that ship was that the women stopped wearing shorts, halters, and swimsuits on deck. They feared that exposed flesh could provoke the pirates to lust and assault.[10]

What does common sense say? Which girl is more likely to be targeted at a party or on a date: one whose body is covered, or one who gives her date an "eyeful" every time she bends over or uncrosses her legs? Men are visually stimulated. After viewing exposed breasts and thighs for several hours, a man may think he is entitled to sex on the way home. A woman who dresses modestly helps to curb her date's lust.

There is common view in academic circles that rape is always about controlling another person and not about sexual desire. We would not argue this point in rapes committed by strangers, but date rape carries a different dimension. One excuse that rapists often give is, "Well, she wore a short skirt," or "She was dressed so hot that I knew she wanted it."

Many people do believe that dress and action contribute to unwanted sexual advances. For instance, a 2005 Amnesty International poll of 1,000 people found over 25 percent believe a woman is at least partly to blame if she has worn sexy or revealing clothing.[11]

The fallacy of this view does not change the fact that people use it as a basis for action. Biblical modesty is the safe course (1 Timothy 2:9). If a woman dresses and acts decorously, she is putting herself in no extra danger. No one would argue that point. And many would argue that she is putting herself at increased risk if she goes on a date or to a place where singles are dressed in revealing and tantalizing clothes.

Don't start a fire with lascivious actions
Some common misconceptions of males perpetrating date rape include the following:

- » She wouldn't go parking with me if she didn't want to have sex.
- » If she did not want to have sex, why did she let me go as far as she did?
- » If she gets me excited, then it is her responsibility to do something about it.
- » If she's aroused, she wants to have sex.

According to the Amnesty International report, one in three people also believes that women who behave flirtatiously are at least partially responsible if they are raped.[12] Again, this is unjustified, but the safer course is to avoid drawing the wrong kind of attention to ourselves. The Bible clearly forbids lascivious actions, including dancing, swimming with a boyfriend, and parking/petting (Galatians 5:19–21).

One convicted date rapist used the phrase "train wreck" to describe his feelings after having engaged in kissing and making out before his date said she wanted to stop. Another described his thoughts in this slang speech:

> And your emotions and your feelings and your/ everything's runnin' to go to there. And when it stops it's just like hittin' a wall. All your emotions have piled up and you're like—you're angry, you're confused, you're upset, you're wantin' ta hurt somethin' or, you know, 'cause they didn't—you didn't get to finish what you was doin'.[13]

The Bible says, "Flee fornication" (1 Corinthians 6:18), which implies that we should not see how close we can get to it without going past the line.

Discussion Questions

1. Is it wise to assume that someone you date has the same views on morals as you do? How does dating a fellow Christian improve the likelihood that you will be safe when dating?

2. What kind of emotional scare tactics might be used to try to coerce you to give in to sexual temptation?

3. If a friend asked your advice about how to handle pressure to commit fornication, what would you suggest? What scriptures would be helpful in making a decision?

4. How important is it to keep a good reputation? How could this help to avoid date rape?

5. Do you think it is wise to tell someone you date about your views of sex? How could this help to prevent an assault?
    a. Is it wise to be alone with a date in an apartment, dorm room, or parent's house? What percentage of rapes take place in such places?
    b. Where is it best to go on dates, and what other advice would you give to help avoid both fornication and sexual assault?

6. If someone makes you feel uncomfortable, how should you handle it?

7. What role, if any, does your clothing play in the potential for date rape? What are some clothing styles that might draw the wrong kind of attention?

8. What role, if any, do your actions play in the potential for date rape? What are three actions/activities that might draw the wrong kind of attention and put you in a vulnerable position?

9. What would you say to a person who said of date rape: "It'll never happen to me."

10. What are some characteristics that you feel are important in a person you want to date? How do these characteristics help lead to safe and enjoyable dates?

CHAPTER 12

DON'T DRINK AND DATE

Lesson text: Proverbs 23:29-35
Memory verse: "Wine is a mocker, strong drink is raging: and whosoever is deceived thereby is not wise" (Proverbs 20:1).

It's a first date. He's nervous and eager to impress her. She's shy but doesn't want him to think she's a prude. They go to a party; their friends are drinking. They want to fit in with the crowd, so they have a few beers. By the end of the date, well, they may have lost respect for one another—and a whole lot more. Drinking is dangerous. Dating is dangerous. Drinking while dating is very dangerous.

Consider these statistics about rape or attempted rape among college students:

» Seven to 25 percent of college males report having forced sexual intercourse with a woman.[4]

» One in twelve college males admits to having committed acts that met rape's legal definition.

» The Florida Institute of Technology reports that one in four college men admits to the use of sexual aggression with women.[5]

» Sixteen percent of the male students who committed rape and 10 percent of those who attempted a rape took part in episodes involving more than one attacker.

Solomon's words are appropriate: "A prudent [woman] foreseeth the evil, and hideth [herself]: but the simple pass on, and are punished [hurt]" (Proverbs 22:3).

We've already discussed the dangers of date rape; add alcohol to the dating scene, and the probablilty of rape increases. Acquaintance or date rape occurs most often during or after social events such as parties at bars, fraternity/sorority parties, or other places where students may congregate while using alcohol or drugs. It can occur on a date, but often it is perpetrated by a member of a social circle who attended the same party.

According to Wikipedia, over 80 percent of date rapes included the use of alcohol by at least one partner, while over 50 percent involved the use by both partners.[1] Another source confirmed the likelihood that alcohol would be involved in a date rape: 75 percent of male and 55 percent of female students in an occurrence of date rape had been drinking or using drugs.[2]

Drinking makes one vulnerable to manipulation and attack

Drinking dulls common sense. Nahum warned that a drunk person makes himself/herself vulnerable to the ungodly: "While they are drunken as drunkards, they shall be devoured as stubble fully dry" (Nahum 1:10; cf. 1 Samuel 30:16–17).

Lot's daughters used alcohol to commit rape (Genesis 19:32–35). Habakkuk warned, "Woe unto him that giveth his neighbour drink, that puttest thy bottle to him, and makest him drunken also, that thou mayest look on their nakedness" (Habakkuk 2:15).

Note how Solomon's list of the dangers of using alcohol in Proverbs 23:29–35 parallel the results of rape:

- » Woe (23:29);
- » Sorrow (23:29);
- » Contentions (23:29);
- » Wounds they can't remember getting (23:29);
- » Feeling like you have been bitten by a snake (23:32);
- » Association with strange (lust-driven, loose) people (23:33)
- » Unable to remember what happened (23:34);
- » Attacked by others while passed out, but unable to remember it (23:35).

Some men are more sinister. They push their dates to drink so they will be unable to resist physical or emotional pressure to have sex. Alcohol remains the drug most frequently implicated in substance-assisted sexual assault. The immoral who want to take advantage of young women often banter about the adage: "Candy is dandy, but liquor is quicker." A college senior warned freshman girls: "Be very wary of guys giving you free alcohol! I mean, if a guy keeps pouring free vodka down your throat, it's not necessarily benevolent . . . he's trying to get you drunk enough to get you to go home with him."

Further, many men and women feel that a woman who has more than one or two drinks is asking for sex, no matter what she says. We know that regardless of how much a woman drinks, however, a man is never justified in forcing sex on her if she resists or says no, or if she is under the influence of alcohol. But in the real world, which girl is most likely to be targeted for rape: one that drinks or one that doesn't? Plainly stated, a teen girl who drinks is making a target of herself.

Drinking loosens inhibitions and moral restraints
King Lemuel warned against drinking alcohol, "Lest they drink, and forget the law" (Proverbs 31:5). David knew this about alcohol and got Uriah drunk so he could get him to do something that his conscience forbade (cf. 2 Samuel 11:8–13). Notice the progression in this sentence about Noah:

- » "And he drank of the wine, and
- » was drunken; and
- » he was uncovered within his tent" (Genesis 9:21).

One college freshman woman wrote: "And it would be like, 'I cannot believe I was with that guy the other night . . . . I did not even know this guy! I have no idea what happened. Sometimes you just wake up next to him or something, and you don't know what happened, and you don't want to ask him.'"

Of course, it is not just men who take advantage of women. There are wild girls who want to take advantage of a man for sexual favors. Solomon spoke of a woman who was set on seducing a man who "mingled her wine"[4] (Proverbs 9:2).

The desire to commit sexual violence may actually cause alcohol consumption, in that a male perpetrator drinks alcohol before committing a sexual assault in order to justify his behavior. Of course the culture among many college-aged males and some fraternities often encourage both heavy drinking and the sexual exploitation of women.

Solomon said that wine mocks and deceives (Proverbs 20:1). Paul warned that in drunkenness there is "excess" (Ephesians 5:18), a word (*asotia*[5]) which means "riot." Riot is associated with theft, pillaging, and rape. One of the excesses of wine is aggressive sexual behavior and decreased moral restraint. Isaiah warns that wine makes men err in judgment and "through strong drink are out of the way; the priest and the prophet have erred through strong drink, they are swallowed up of wine, they are out of the way through strong drink; they err in vision, they stumble in judgment" (Isaiah 28:7).

Drinking leads to aggressive behavior

Solomon said, "Strong drink is raging" (Proverbs 20:1). It allows aggressive tendencies to surface. It inflames (Isaiah 5:11). Alcohol impairs judgment and makes some people much more aggressive than they normally are.

A drunk man will say (threaten) and do (rape) things he would not do sober. A male college junior, who for obvious reasons chose to remain anonymous, said,

> When I woke up, she was crying, and we both were shocked and unsure about what had happened. I've lived with that experience

ever since. For months afterwards, I was depressed and frightened. I dropped out of school for a semester. I know she's suffered. If people knew how awful it is to take advantage of someone and live with yourself afterwards they would act very differently.

The Bible is right when it says a man who commits sex sin will get "a wound and dishonour" and "his reproach shall not be wiped away" (Proverbs 6:33).

Men who drink are at greater risk of being accused—rightly or wrongly—of raping someone. If a girl is intoxicated, she cannot consent to sex and the male could be charged with rape. It does not matter whether he knew she was intoxicated; it doesn't matter if he was also intoxicated; all that matters is that she was not in a state of mind to consent, and therefore it is classified as rape. If a man gets a girl drunk or high and then has sex with her, he has committed sexual assault. If you do not want to be arrested as a rapist, then do not become intoxicated while at a party or on a date.

Solomon warns that when a man is intoxicated his "eyes shall behold strange women, and thine heart shall utter perverse things" (Proverbs 23:33). A "strange" woman is what we would call a "loose" woman. Adam Clarke commented on this verse: "Evil concupiscence (lust) is inseparable from drunkenness" (cf. Romans 13:13).

Take the threat of rape seriously

Some young women tune out information about rape with a dismissive, "It'll never happen to me." Solomon said, "A wise man [woman] feareth, and departeth from evil: but the fool rageth, and is confident" (Proverbs 14:16).

There is a very real chance that you could become the victim of rape. Date rape is one of the fastest growing crimes among college-age Americans (cf. Hebrews 13:4).

» Sexual violence has now surpassed theft as the number one security concern at U.S. universities.

» A national survey indicated that 15 percent of women students on college campuses will become victims of rape, and 11 percent will be victims of attempted rape.[16]

- » Of 1,000 representative female students at a large urban university, over half had experienced some form of unwanted sex. Twelve percent of these acts were perpetrated by casual dates and 43 percent by steady dating partners.[17]

- » According to the University of Florida police (one of the largest campuses in the nation), 84 percent of women who were raped knew their assailants[18] (this figure is consistent with nation-wide figures).

Whether you are a man or woman, drinking alcohol reduces four skills that can protect you. These skills form the word *RAPE:*

- » **R** ealize what situations place you in danger of committing rape or being a victim of rape;

- » **A** void and manage conflicts with partners and intimates;

- » **P** erceive clearly what others are doing; and

- » **E** stablish and communicate your desires and limits about sex.[7]

Here is just one more reason not to break God's law on drugs, including alcohol.

We hasten to add that there are many honorable young men and woman who have a great desire for sexual purity. Date those who sincerely share your faith, and you will have a wonderful experience dating until you find that special person with whom you want to spend the rest of your life.

Discussion Questions

1. Why is dating and drinking a dangerous combination?
   a. How widespread is the problem of sexual assault on college campuses? (Compare this to what you see in high school—is it more or less?)
   b. Comment on this sentence: "Plainly stated, a teen girl who drinks is making a target of herself."

2. Are most rapes committed by strangers or acquaintances? In how many of those cases is alcohol involved?

3. What application does this verse have to the potential for date rape: "A prudent man [woman] foreseeth the evil, and hideth himself [herself]: but the simple pass on, and are punished [hurt]"? (Proverbs 22:3).

4. Explain how some college men violate Habakkuk 2:15: "Woe unto him that giveth his neighbour drink, that puttest thy bottle to him, and makest him drunken also, that thou mayest look on their nakedness."

5. How does Noah's experience parallel many who have been sexually assaulted today: "And he drank of the wine, and was drunken; and he was uncovered within his tent"? (Genesis 9:21).

6. What common misconceptions exist among fraternity house boys toward girls? How can they protect themselves from attack and manipulation?

7. What does the Bible mean when it says that
    a. Wine mocks? (Proverbs 20:1).
    b. Wine deceives? (Proverbs 20:1).
    c. In drunkenness there is "excess"? (Ephesians 6:18).
    d. "Strong drink is raging"? (Proverbs 20:1).
    e. Alcohol leads to wounds one can't remember getting? (Proverbs 23:29).
    f. Alcohol leads to attack while passed out? (Proverbs 23:35).
    g. Wine inflames? (Isaiah 5:11).

8. How hard would it be to live with having been raped? How hard would it be to live with knowing you had assaulted someone while under the influence of alcohol?

9. Read Proverbs 23:29–35 and give an example of how each of these verses happens today. (For example, "Who hath woe?"

A teen drinks and drives and wrecks his car. He has trouble he would not have had if he had left alcohol alone.)

10. What four steps can one take to protect himself/herself? (Use the letters R-A-P-E.)

CHAPTER 13

WAIT TILL THE HONEYMOON?

Lesson text: Genesis 39:1–20
Memory Verse: "Marriage is honorable in all, and the bed undefiled: but whoremongers and adulterers God will judge" (Hebrews 13:4).

Remember what we said in Chapter 1 about sin as a thief? Sin can steal innocence and purity. God created the pleasure of sexual union; it is a blessing intended for a man and woman to share in marriage. One young woman confessed, "My one wish would be that I could be a virgin again. I can't think of anything more wonderful than being a virgin on my wedding night." Though sexual sin can be forgiven, innocence can't be restored.

If you remain a virgin until your wedding night, it will not be accidental. It will be because you made up your mind to wait so your future mate could unwrap a gift that no one ever had before—and that no one can ever have in the same way. At least 75 percent of high school students in one poll (including mostly sexually active students) said they "wanted to marry a virgin."[1] If you keep yourself pure, you will be far more desirable when it comes time to marry.

Today, young people are being rushed into making sexual decisions by the time they barely reach puberty. Counseling programs used to be geared to high school and college students; now they start in junior high. About one million teens become pregnant each year in the United States, according to the Medical Institute for Sexual Health. Estimates suggest ten times that number are sexually active. One-third of teen pregnancies result in abortions. Of the children carried to term, about 72 percent are born out of wedlock.

Congress has recognized the crisis of teenage sexuality. Every year, a staggering ten billion dollars is spent on fighting the major sexually transmitted diseases (STDs) and their preventable complications (not including AIDS-based programs). Congress has seen the relative failure of the "safe sex" approach, and from 1997 until recently has appropriated new funds under a program called Title V, which distributes grants for abstinence-based education.

Although there is great pressure on young people to be sexually active, it is possible to wait until the wedding night (Romans 12:2). Joseph is an excellent example of how to remain a virgin when tempted to become sexually active (Genesis 39:1–20). After being sold into slavery in Egypt, he became the head of Potiphar's household and the object of Potiphar's wife's passions. Though still young and unmarried, he withstood her regular advances. One day she grabbed him by his coat to force him to be with her. He ran from her, leaving his coat in her hand. What does Joseph teach us?

Don't let anyone pressure you into sin (Genesis 39:7–9)

Mrs. Potiphar tried to force Joseph to do what he knew was wrong. Hundreds of young people were asked why they were having premarital sex. Seventy-nine percent said it was to "fit in and be cool" (only one answered "because I'm in love," and only boys said "because it feels good"). Some felt they had no other choice. If they wanted to maintain a steady relationship, they had to go to another level. Young person, you control what happens to your body.

Say no and mean it. Peter and John told some officials, "Whether it be right in the sight of God to hearken unto you more than unto God, judge ye" (Acts 4:19). Like them, don't let anybody pressure you. It doesn't matter if he's two years older than you, and you waited a year for him to ask you out. It doesn't matter if she's drop-dead gorgeous, and every guy in school wants to be with her. It doesn't matter if you've dated for two years and plan on getting married one day. Forget the locker room questions. He has no right to pressure you. She has no right to expect you to sin with her.

If you choose to wait, you are not alone. Teen pregnancies—although still far too high—have decreased this decade because more and more teens choose to remain virgins. Government officials are amazed at the success of many abstinence-based programs. (One in Rhea County, Tennessee, for instance, saw that county drop from being number one in teen pregnancies per capita in the state to sixty-fourth in just two years.) If your date pressures you, remember that lust is selfish; love is self-sacrificing. True friends respect each other's convictions.

Joseph could have said, "If I want to keep my job, I'd better do what my 'owner' wants," but he did not because he had already made up his mind about his sexual boundaries. Young people must decide how far they will go before ever leaving on a date. Don't say, "I'm not sure yet; I'll decide later." Bad decisions are made after you've been kissing. Cold facts lose their chill in the heat of the moment. When passion runs strong, reason gets run over. You can do something in half an hour you'll regret for the rest of your life. Joshua said, "Choose you this day whom ye will serve" (Joshua 24:15). Like the Hebrew teens in a foreign culture, each teen today must "purpose in his heart" not to defile himself/herself (Daniel 1:8; cf. Proverbs 11:22; 1 Thessalonians 4:1–5; James 1:8).

Recognize you are under surveillance (Genesis 39:9)
How many would undress and go all the way if they knew their father was watching from the next room? Sexual encounters usually happen—by design—in places far from any watchful eyes. The day Mrs. Potiphar tempted Joseph, he was a long way from home. Probably no one would have ever known what happened on Potiphar's couch that afternoon. Except one.

Joseph knew that the two of them were not as alone as she thought. God watched from heaven. Joseph asked her, "How then can I do this great wickedness, and sin against God?" (Genesis 39:9).

Our father might not see us, but our Father will. "All things are naked and opened unto the eyes of him" (Hebrews 4:13). On the last day, "God shall judge the secrets of men by Jesus Christ" (Romans 2:16; cf. 2 Corinthians 5:10). God watches, but He doesn't sit as a tyrant issuing rules to ruin our fun. God invented sex in the first place; He wants us to enjoy sexual satisfaction (Proverbs 5:18–19). God is not against sex; He just wants the time to be right. The right time is when we are married—and never before. "Marriage is honourable in all, and the bed undefiled: but whoremongers and adulterers God will judge" (Hebrews 13:4).

Sex outside the limits is dangerous. God also invented fire and water, but He doesn't want us to be burned or drowned. As a wise and loving Father, He sees the misery that waits around the corner (Proverbs 7:26–27). He wants His children to avoid sleepless nights, tear-soaked pillows, diseased bodes, and wounded souls (Isaiah 59:1–2). He says, "I don't want you to have sex outside of marriage because I know it will break your heart, and when you hurt, I do, too."

The key to remaining strong is keeping a clean mind. Thomas K. Beecher found that a church clock was habitually too fast or too slow. He hung a sign beside it which read, "Don't blame the hands—the trouble lies deeper." If you or your date has problems keeping "all hands on deck," he or she has a heart problem, not a hand problem. Actions follow thoughts (Mark 7:20–23; Ephesians 4:22–24; Philippians 4:8; Titus 1:15), just as consequences follow actions. The Bible warns, "Be sure your sin will find you out" (Numbers 32:23). If we fill our minds with R-rated movies, worldly magazines, and filthy romance novels; if we constantly watch videos or visit Web sites with half-naked people doing indecent things to each other, then the temptation to experiment sexually will be strong.

Avoid compromising situations (Genesis 39:10–11)
Joseph found himself in a bad position—alone with a sinful woman. Sin pursues those who try to do right (Genesis 4:7; Proverbs 7:21). The devil

seeks souls (1 Peter 5:8). Peter sinned while he was warming by the wrong fire (Luke 22:54–57), and if we feed the fire, we're likely to get burned, too. Solomon asked, "Can a man take fire in his bosom, and his clothes not be burned?" (Proverbs 6:27).

In order to withstand temptation, we must stay out of places where it is possible (even easy) to have sex. Most premarital sexual encounters occur while drinking alcohol, which lowers inhibitions (Proverbs 20:1), after dancing, which heightens sexual desire (Galatians 5:19), or while petting in parked cars, which is nothing less than sexual foreplay (1 Peter 2:11). If you want to stay pure for the honeymoon, don't park in a secluded place "to listen to music." When you return from a date, say goodnight at the door—don't invite him into your empty apartment to "watch TV." Think ahead. Say no and mean it.

Know when to run (Genesis 39:12)

Joseph knew when to stand and fight and when to turn and run. This was a time to try out the running shoes! God says to "flee fornication" (1 Corinthians 6:18) and "flee also youthful lusts" (2 Timothy 2:22). *Flee* means to "run away; shun; vanish; escape." *Lusts* here means "a longing for what is forbidden, unbridled passion, sexual desire." A person is foolish who sees how close he or she can get without "going all the way."

Girls, if you have to walk home in order to keep your virginity, then walk (or call someone to get you). Guys, if things are getting out of hand, take her home early. If you have to break off a relationship to keep from having sex, break up. It's not real love that leads down that path. It is better to sit at home a few weeks than to defile your body (1 Corinthians 6:18) and jeopardize your soul (1 Corinthians 6:9–10).

Eternity in heaven is worth more than a few minutes of pleasure (Galatians 5:19–21). No relationship with a boyfriend or girlfriend is worth trading fellowship with Jesus and His Father. Run away from sin.

Remember the rewards and costs (Genesis 39:2–5, 21, 23)

God blessed Joseph for waiting—he later married a leader's daughter (Genesis 41:45, 50). God blesses those who save themselves today (Matthew 5:8;

19:4–6; Revelation 21:27). On the other hand, the promiscuous invite a host of problems home with them. They face the very real chance of getting a disease. A person can get at least twenty-five different diseases by having sex with someone. It can happen on the first time—4,219 teens a day get an STD. Remember, you are not just going to bed with this person, but with every other person he or she has ever been with. Think about how that fact increases the odds of getting a disease!

Most sexually active teen girls said they did not "know him well enough" to ask whether he had been with others or if he had a disease. They knew him well enough to take off their clothes and sleep with him, but not well enough to open their hearts and talk with him! What's wrong with this picture? Five of the top ten reportable infectious diseases—including the top three and four of the top five—are sexually transmitted.[2] Adolescents (10–19) and young adults (20–24) are the age groups most at risk for acquiring an STD. Some STDs are incurable and all are extremely embarrassing. (Picture yourself going to the doctor or telling your parents.) Ask someone with herpes or AIDS if the sex was worth it. No!

Further, the guilt and shame of unmarried sex takes its toll on the mind and soul. Don't underestimate it. (Have you ever noticed that teen suicide and promiscuity levels rise together?) Then there is the danger of pregnancy, and often pressure to kill the baby by abortion (Proverbs 6:17). Girls, don't think he'll stay around if you get pregnant. The cold truth is that he'll probably drop you as soon as he finds out—or at least within a month.

Ministers have counseled pregnant girls who cried till they couldn't cry any more often enough to know what happens in the real world. Of those who do opt to marry, the union usually ends in a divorce within two years. Marriage is hard enough without having to start off caring for—and paying for—a baby. Don't say it won't happen to you. It happens a million times a year (2,740 times a day) to some girl and boy just like you. Don't trade sin's momentary pleasure for its long-lasting unhappy consequences (Hebrews 11:25).

It is easy to see why God does not want sex outside of marriage for His children. He wants us to enjoy our young years (Ecclesiastes 11:9), and be happy and fulfilled throughout life (John 10:10; Philippians 4:4). Sin's pigpen is hard to leave (Luke 15:11–19); God's love is hard to dismiss (Luke 15:20–24). Give God your soul and body!

P.S.

If you are already sexually active, please stop immediately. You can't undo the past, but you can correct the future. You may not yet be pregnant or have a disease. Your future marriage partner will thank you. God will forgive you: "The Lord your God is gracious and merciful, and will not turn away his face from you, if ye return unto him" (2 Chronicles 30:9). To be forgiven of sin initially—all sin!—one must believe in Jesus as the Son of God (John 3:16), repent of sin (Luke 13:3), confess Christ (Romans 10:9–10), and be baptized to have past sins washed away (Acts 22:16). When Christians sin, they must repent of it, confess it to the church (if known to others), and pray to God to forgive it (Acts 8:22; James 5:16; 1 John 1:7–10).

If you already have a child on the way, please don't abort the baby. If you can't keep the child, please let a loving family adopt it. If you already have a child outside of marriage, love him or her with all your heart. Your child is one of God's children, too, and He loves him or her even more than you do. Do your best to live right from now on. God will bless you, and His people will help in as many ways as they can.

Discussion Questions

1. Who pressures teens today to become sexually active? Why is it difficult to stand firm against this pressure? Discuss strategies for the teens in this class to overcome these pressures (what kind of people to date, what to say when the subject comes up, places to go, places not to go, and so forth.)

2. It would have been easy for Joseph to give in to Mrs. Potiphar's advances; she tempted him "day by day"—not just once. What reasons did Joseph give for saying no to her?

3. Often worldly people who advocate sex education in the schools laugh at the idea of teaching sexual abstinence to teens. What evidence exists that teaching abstinence works?

4. Who should really feel ashamed: one who is keeping himself/herself sexually pure, or one who has not? Who then should feel embarrassed about the subject—the Christian or the worldly person? (Keep this fact in mind when someone wants to make fun of your virginity.)

5. The key to remaining strong is keeping a clean mind. How can Christian teens keep their minds clean so they can live pure lives? What contributes to a dirty mind?

6. Would teens be likely to have sex if they knew their parents were watching? How can knowing their heavenly Father sees everything they do help teens to stay strong?

7. In 1 Corinthians 10:13, God promises that He will provide a way to escape the temptations we face. How did Joseph escape his temptation with Mrs. Potiphar? How can teens today escape sexual temptation?

8. God gives us rules for our protection. What protections do we have when we obey God and save sex for marriage as God intended?

9. An unmarried couple may say, "We're not hurting anyone by having sex." Is that true? Who may be hurt by their actions?

10. If teenagers are already sexually active but come to understand that they are sinning, what should they do to make things right?

CHAPTER 14

PORNOGRAPHY'S PAIN

Lesson text: Proverbs 6:20–28
Memory verse: "Blessed are the pure in heart: for they shall see God" (Matthew 5:8).

An anonymous reader asked a preacher this question: "Shouldn't a person have the right to watch or read whatever he pleases? As long as he watches or reads in the privacy of his own home, and nobody gets hurt, what difference does it make?"

This view of pornography is commonly held among many American males—and some females. Is it true, or is it another example of Satan's deceit? Let's consider who is hurt by pornography's use.

Pornography hurts the user

The individual who reads and watches pornography does not come away unscathed. Paul wrote, "Be not deceived; God is not mocked: for whatsoever a man soweth, that shall he also reap. For he that soweth to his flesh shall of the flesh reap corruption; but he that soweth to the Spirit shall of the Spirit reap life everlasting" (Galatians 6:7–8). God promises one will reap "corruption;"[1] who could dare disagree with Him?

What a person sows in his mind determines how he acts. Solomon wrote, "For as he thinketh in his heart, so is he" (Proverbs 23:7), and, "Keep thy heart with all diligence; for out of it are the issues of life" (Proverbs 4:23). Someone observed, "Sow a thought, reap an action. Sow an action, reap a character. Sow a character, reap a destiny."

Like alcohol and drugs, pornography is undeniably addictive. The percentage of people addicted to pornography is reaching epidemic numbers.[2] According to an MSNBC survey, 10 percent of respondents indicated they are addicted to sex or Internet pornography.[3] Other estimates range from 3–8 percent, which would indicate that at least 8.7 million Americans are addicted to pornography—the number may be as high as 29 million.[4] Sex addiction is not gender specific, as one might imagine. Half of cyber sex addicts are men, and half are women, with men preferring pornography pictures and women preferring sexually explicit chat rooms. However, 23 percent of women preferred pictures.[5]

Why is pornography addictive? Beyond the obvious—that it partially satisfies the human sex drive—Dr. Alvin Cooper, clinical director of the San Jose Marital Services and Sexuality Center in San Jose, California, found that people engage in online sexual activities to break away from their daily routines, explore fantasies, relieve stress, and spice up their sex lives.

Like alcohol and drugs, pornography is undeniably progressive. Though it may start small, someone has aptly described it as "athlete's foot of the mind." It never goes away. It always asks to be scratched, promising relief. To scratch, however, is to cause pain and to intensify the itch. It progresses to greater amounts of time devoted to it, and it progresses to greater perversions—more extreme types of pornography. The user needs rougher and more sexually shocking material to achieve the same level of satisfaction each time. For example, simple "swimsuit porn" turns to more daring pictures, then to pictures of younger and younger girls. Eventually, the user may turn to deviant sexual content, seeking more intense satisfaction.

Pornography hurts women

The Bible commands men to honor women (1 Peter 3:7). This concept is sadly lost in a modern world. Women are viewed by many men as nothing more than sex objects. Pornography cheapens women and makes them vulnerable to men who abandon self restraint to feed the beast of forcible sex.

The National Victim Center now estimates that at least one woman is raped in the U.S. every forty-six seconds.[6] Why so many rapes? Many experts point to the increased use of pornography.

» Exposure to pornography increases the inclination to believe that women like to be hurt, to be humiliated, to be forced to do things that they do not want to do, or to pretend to be forced to do things that they really do want to do. Researchers reported that in the field of violent/pornographic movies, prolonged exposure to X-rated as well as R-rated films caused male college students to be "desensitized" to rape and violence, and more accepting to the rape-myth that women say no when they really mean yes.[7]

» Dr. Sal Pellicano, veteran prison chaplain for prison systems in Florida, North Carolina, and New Jersey, reports that during his fifteen-year career, 100 percent of the inmates he has known who have been incarcerated for a sex crime were pornography users.[8]

» A study released by the University of New Hampshire revealed that states with the highest readership of porn magazines such as *Playboy* and *Hustler* also had the highest rape rates. Researchers Murray Straus and Larry Baron also found "an unusually high correlation" between sex magazine readership and the rape rate in all states. They stated, "The fact that sex magazine readership is strongly and consistently correlated with rape supports the theory that porn endorses attitudes that increase the likelihood of rape."[9]

A person may think he/she has the "right" to view pornorgraphy as an "innocent" pastime, but playing with such strong desires often turns violent and leads to broken lives, having one's name on a sex offender's Web site, and time spent in prison. The women who are victimized often have serious lifelong issues that can be traced back to someone "innocently" viewing a porn site or picking up a "men's magazine."

Pornography hurts children

The next time someone says that pornography is an innocent pastime, remind him or her that pornography is the driving force behind the rampant child abuse that ruins countless innocent lives each year. Consider some of the startling facts:

- » Human Development Specialist Dr. Shirley O'Brien of the University of Arizona found that child pornography victimizes as many as 600,000 children in the United States each year. Victims often include children as young as three and as old as eighteen.[10]

- » The typical serial child molester will abuse more than 360 victims over the course of his lifetime. He is usually able to abuse 30 to 60 children before he is caught the first time.[11]

- » Among female adolescents who had sex before age fourteen, 74 percent reported that it was involuntary.[12]

- » It is estimated that one in three girls and one in seven boys are sexually molested by age eighteen.[13]

Pornography hurts society

An estimated 3,500–5,000 people in the U.S. are murdered each year by "recreational killers."[14] Most of them feed on pornography. Serial killer Ted Bundy, in an interview just before his execution, said,

> Listen, I'm no social scientist, and I haven't done a survey. I don't pretend that I know what John Q. Citizen thinks about this. But I've lived in prison for a long time now. And I've met a lot of men who were motivated to commit violence just like me. And without

exception, without question, every one of them was deeply involved in pornography. There's no question about it. The FBI's own study on serial homicide shows that the most common interest among serial killers is pornography. Well-meaning, decent people will condemn the behavior of a Ted Bundy, while they're walking past a magazine rack full of the very kinds of things that send young kids down the road to be Ted Bundys. But I'll tell you, there are lots of other kids playing in streets around this country today who are going to be dead tomorrow, and the next day, and the next day and month, because other young people are reading the kinds of things and seeing the kinds of things that are available in the media today. (For the text of the interview with Dr. James Dobson, see http://www.pureintimacy.org/online1/bundy.html).

Is it any wonder that the Bible instructs Christians to think on that which is pure? Paul wrote, "Finally brethren, whatsoever things are true, whatsoever things are honest, whatsoever things are just, whatsoever things are pure, whatsoever things are lovely, whatsoever things are of good report; if there be any virtue, and if there be any praise, think on these things" (Philippians 4:8; cf. 2 Corinthians 10:5). Wayne Jackson notes, "Pornography, sexually explicit movies, etc., have paved the way for many an act of rape, adultery, incest, homosexuality, and other equally vile sins . . . One simply cannot feed upon the impure and be pure!" (Matthew 5:28; 2 Peter 2:14).

Discussion Questions

1. If you know someone who looks at pornography in magazines or on the Internet, he or she might ask you, "Shouldn't a person have the right to watch or read whatever he or she pleases?" How would you answer this question?

2. How does pornography hurt the user? How does it hurt women, children, and society in general?

3. Are you feeling overwhelmed by the statistics about pornography? Try plugging in real people to the numbers.

   a. For example, "Among teenage girls, 30 percent said they had been sexually harassed in a chat room." Do you know ten teenage girls who go online? Chances are, three of them have been sexually harassed in a chat room—and maybe you are one of them.

   b. Or think about this one: "Ninety-one percent of the first exposure by a teen to pornography was during benign activities, such as research for school projects or surfing the Web for other information." (Pornographic Web sites often disguise themselves by using common search terms used by children, such as names of popular teen games, TV shows, or action figures.) Do you know ten teenagers who use the Web for research projects? At least nine of them have accidentally stumbled onto a porn site.

4. Ninety-five percent of 15- to 17-year-old teens go online; 83 percent have Internet access from home; and 29 percent have Internet access in their bedroom. Yet only 33 percent of teens have a filtering service on Internet at home and 43 percent of teens do not have rules at home about Internet use. What safeguards do you have to prevent that on your computer? Is your computer screen facing a public area in your home? Does your computer have an Internet filter? Do you have a personal rule about immediately closing any screen that has objectionable material?

5. Review the statistics about children and the Internet. Do you have younger brothers and sisters who might be affected? How can you teach them to be safe from pornography?

CHAPTER 15

BET YOU DIDN'T KNOW THIS ABOUT LOTTERIES

Lesson text: Proverbs 16:22

Memory verse: "Wherefore be ye not unwise, but understanding what the will of the Lord is" (Ephesians 5:17).

M ost teens don't have as much money as they'd like. They don't throw money to the wind or spend frivolously. They pinch pennies, collect quarters, and stretch dollars. They buy sale items and spend more time in Wal-Mart, Costco, and Target than in Dillard's, Sears, and Macy's.

To put hard-earned money up for grabs is not something they do lightly. To push a Jackson across a countertop and not get a bag of something in return does not set right. To walk away leaving Lincoln or even Washington behind is just not something they would normally do. And Mr. Franklin doesn't come out except on very special occasions.

Until it comes to lottery tickets. Then the rules no longer apply. Did you know that Americans gamble more money each year than they spend on groceries? The devil disguises greed as the opportunity to "win big" or "get lucky." The idea of winning millions by spending a dollar or two is exciting, but that's not the whole story when it comes to playing the lottery.

Some Bible Verses to Consider

When it comes to the chances of winning the lottery, a person is either in the group that believes it is absolutely impossible or in the group that believes one has a very good chance, so why not play? Which one is right?

Keep in mind that the Bible forbids us to be unwise—which is another way of saying, "Don't be foolish" or "Do not act stupidly." Paul wrote, "Wherefore be ye not unwise, but understanding what the will of the Lord is" (Ephesians 5:17). "Fools hate knowledge" but a wise person searches out a matter (Proverbs 1:22; cf. Job 29:16; Proverbs 13:16; 25:2). "The wisdom of the prudent is to understand his way" (Proverbs 14:8). "Understanding is a wellspring of life unto him that hath it: but the instruction of fools is folly" (Proverbs 16:22).

We are to watch our step in questionable matters. Paul wrote that we are to "walk circumspectly" (carefully) (Ephesians 5:15), and walk wisely among those outside the church (Colossians 4:5). We should inform ourselves with the facts and then make correct and good decisions.

How Lotteries Work

Lotteries are games in which contestants match their chosen set of numbers with a winning set. The classic lottery is a drawing in which each contestant buys a combination of numbers. Each combination of numbers, or "play," is usually priced at $1. Plays are usually non-exclusive, meaning that two or more ticket holders may buy the same combination. The lottery organization then draws the winning combination of 5–8 numbers, usually from 1 to 50, using a randomized, automatic ball tumbler machine. To win, contestants match their combinations of numbers with the drawn combination.

Misconceptions about lotteries

Numbers will eventually come up. The three most common lottery products are instant (scratch-off) games, numbers games, and Lotto. To win the grand prize in a typical Lotto game, a player buys a one-dollar ticket and must correctly match six numbers drawn randomly without replacement from, say, forty-four numbers. This is called a 6/44 game.

There is no more chance that playing the same lottery numbers every week for a year will make them come up more than any other numbers will. You may as well play random numbers every time. Even if you play the same numbers every day, it may take more than 35,000 years to guarantee a win.

An obscure lottery is better. Most states have state-sponsored and multi-state lotteries. Only eight states have no state or interstate lotteries: Alabama, Alaska, Arkansas, Hawaii, Mississippi, Nevada, Utah, and Wyoming. Most states participate in multi-state lotteries. Multi-state lotteries generally have larger jackpots, due to the greater number of tickets sold. The Powerball and Mega Millions lotteries are the biggest multi-state lotteries in terms of numbers of participating states.

A common misconception of those playing the lottery is that you have more chances to win in an obscure lottery since fewer people are playing, than on the national jackpot where millions are buying tickets. The truth is that your odds of winning are connected to the numbers you play, not to how many people are buying tickets.

In the United States, you have 1 in 120,526,770 chances of winning the Powerball, and 1 in 135,145,920 chances of winning the Mega Millions. These numbers are fixed every time the lottery is running. The number of people playing is irrelevant, except that you might have to split the jackpot with one or more people if they also picked the winning numbers. The Mega Millions is especially difficult because the drawing order is as important as the numbers drawn. This means the last number to be picked, the Powerball, must also be the last number picked by the player.

Buying more tickets really helps. Buying several tickets does little to increase your chances of winning the lottery. If you buy two tickets, you now have two chances in 135,145,920, but the numbers remain the same. Of course, you would not be able to convince some of this point. Their attitude is, "Don't confuse me with the facts. I've already made up my mind." Solomon spoke of the kind: "A fool hath no delight in understanding" (Proverbs 18:2).

You will get all the money they advertise. Lesser prizes are often awarded for matching fewer than six of the numbers. Lottery agencies take out from 40 to 50 percent of each dollar bet, some of which covers operating costs. The rest is turned over to the state.

The payout changes from week to week. If $20 million is bet on a Lotto jackpot, the state will take between 40 and 50 percent out of that figure immediately. From the half left, smaller prizes are deducted. In most cases, you are left with something like $5 to $8 million for winning a 14 million to 1 bet. And if 20 million people play, it is likely two people will win. So they will have to split that pot. If there are multiple winners, they split the winnings, also known as the Jackpot. Winnings are currently subject to federal income taxes, just like ordinary income. Winnings can be awarded as a yearly annuity or as a lump sum, depending on lottery rules.

A million-dollar prize means you get a million dollars. Most lotteries boast multimillion dollar winnings, which often entices people to spend even more on tickets. However, if you win a million dollar jackpot, you don't actually get a big check for a million dollars. In most cases, the state pays a fraction of the amount to an insurance company, which pays out the interest they gain over a span of time. So rather than a million dollars, you might get a check for $50,000 a year for 20 years or some other period of time.

To pay a winner a million dollars in 20 years, the state only needs to invest $425,700 at a hypothetical rate of 10 percent interest to fulfill its obligation. An amount of $425,700 is quite different from a million in a lump sum. If you had $425,700, and you could invest it at the same hypothetical rate of 10 percent, you could set up your own fund and give yourself more than $50,000 a year. (Of course, 10 percent interest rate would be a generous assumption).

Many who gamble have no idea what the odds are that they will ever win more than they put in. One out of three people in the United States think winning the lottery is the only way to become financially secure in life. They have no idea that they are participating in the biggest hoax of America. James Dobson, founder of Focus on the Family and a member of the National Council on Gambling calls the lottery "the most pernicious form of gambling." Solomon said, "O ye simple, understand wisdom: and, ye fools, be ye of an understanding heart" (Proverbs 8:5).

Odd Odds to Bet On

Most gamblers believe that they have a fairly good chance of winning the lottery at some point in their lives. The gambling industry and the government like to leave this impression. For instance, gambling establishments advertise how much an individual won—they never advertise how much the majority lost. Like liquor advertisers, they do not tell the other side of the story. Lotteries also mislead citizens about the odds of winning, often advertising the top prize while giving the odds for winning any prize—which, in many cases, turns out to be just another lottery ticket.[1]

In some ways it is an oxymoron to talk about lottery "winners" at all. *The New York Post* recently reported: "About once a month on average, a hapless millionaire winner of one of the 37 state lotteries goes bust and files for bankruptcy, experts say. That's the rags-to-rags fate of about one-third of all winners."[2]

Individual rationality is put to the test in gambling. The probability of any ticket winning the jackpot in 6/44 game is 1 out of 7,059,052. In order to win 6/49 Lotto-style game, you have to match six numbers picked at random out of a 49-number universe. The odds of doing this are nearly 1 in 14 million.

The odds of winning a big lottery with a real cash value of $10 million are 1 in 146,107,962. The entire population of the United States is a little over 300,000,000, so you have two chances out of all the people in America. The odds of winning the recent well-publicized lottery prize of more than 300 million dollars are even more staggering.

If you wanted to buy one lottery ticket for every possible combination you would have to purchase 175,711,536 tickets. Thus, to ensure a winner, you would have to pay $10 million more than you would receive through the cash option—not to mention that someone else might also have a winning ticket.

You have a better chance of getting 27 heads in a row flipping a coin.[3] You have a better chance of contracting both the human version of mad cow disease (1 in 40,000,000) and SARS in the United States (1 in 100,000,000).

But let's consider a "regular" lottery

The odds of winning an average lottery are about 1 in 15 million.[4] How likely is it that your number will come up in your lifetime?

Let's illustrate it. If you want to win $1 million for $1, play a single number on a roulette wheel and win. Put all the winnings on another single number and win again. Do it again. And again. You will have just over $1 million. The odds of doing this are about 1 in 2 million.

» You have a 50 percent better chance of being struck by lightening than winning a lottery. In fact, you have a greater chance of getting not only struck but also killed by lightning.

» You have a better chance of being injured by your toilet bowl cleaner.[5]

» You are about 50 times more likely to die from flesh-eating bacteria than winning a lottery.

» If you drive 10 miles to purchase your lottery ticket, it is eleven times more likely for you to be killed in a car accident along the way than for you to win the jackpot.[6]

Compared to winning a lottery, you are more likely to

» Become president of the United States: 10,000,000 to 1

» Die from parts falling off an airplane: 10,000,000 to 1

» Die from a venomous animal or plant: 3,441,325 to 1

» Die from a lightning strike: 2,320,000 to 1.

A person has a better chance of ALL the following things happening to him, than he does of winning the lottery:

- Finding a four-leaf clover on the first try: 1 in 10,000
- Dating a supermodel: 1 in 88,000
- Dating a millionaire: 1 in 215
- Dying by burning nightwear: 1,249,356 to 1

- Writing a *New York Times* best seller: 220 to 1
- Being murdered: 1 in 18,000
- Getting away with murder: 1 in 2
- Being attacked by a dog: 1 in 131,890
- Dying from a dog bite: 1 in 700,000
- A first marriage will survive without separation or divorce for 15 years: 1 in 1.3
- A celebrity marriage will last a lifetime: 1 in 3
- Being on plane with a drunken pilot: 1 in 117
- Dying in an airplane accident: 1 in 354,319
- Being audited by the IRS: 1 in 175
- Having your identity stolen: 1 in 200
- Finding out your child is a genius: 1 in 250
- Becoming a pro athlete: 1 in 22,000
- Catching a ball at a major league ball game: 1 in 563
- One in military winning the Medal of Honor: 1 in 11,000
- Earth will experience a catastrophic collision with an asteroid in the next 100 years: 1 in 5,560
- Dying in such a collision: 1 in 20,000
- Experiencing an earthquake: 1 in 100,000
- Dying in a terrorist attack in a foreign country: 1 in 650,000
- Dying from a car accident: 1 in 18,585
- Dying from accidental drowning: 1 in 79,065
- American home having ice cream in the freezer: 9 in 10.
- American man developing cancer in his lifetime: 1 in 2
- American woman developing cancer in her lifetime: 1 in 3
- Getting prostate cancer: 1 in 6
- Getting breast cancer: 1 in 9
- Being injured shaving: 1 in 6,585
- Being injured using a chain saw: 1 in 4,464
- Being injured mowing the lawn: 1 in 3,623
- Drowning in a bathtub: 1 in 685,000
- Being the victim of serious crime in your lifetime: 1 in 20.

In fact, about the only thing I can find that has higher odds is having your home hit by a meteor: 1 in 182 trillion.

"O ye simple, understand wisdom: and, ye fools, be ye of an understanding heart" (Proverbs 8:5).

Discussion Questions

1. Is it a sin to act stupidly, such as throwing money away on a lottery? (Consider Ephesians 5:17 in your answer.)

2. How do these verses apply to buying lottery tickets?
   a. "Fools hate knowledge but a wise person searches out a matter" (Proverbs 1:22).
   b. "The wisdom of the prudent is to understand his way" (Proverbs 14:8).
   c. "Understanding is a wellspring of life unto him that hath it: but the instruction of fools is folly" (Proverbs 16:22).

3. What are some common misconceptions about lotteries?

4. List some of the things that are more likely to happen than a person winning a lottery.

5. What do you think God thinks of a person spending the money that God gave him/her on lottery tickets? (cf.1 Corinthians 4:2).

CHAPTER 16

LAUNCH OUT WITH JESUS

Lesson text: Luke 5:1–11 (read at start of class)
Memory verse: "Then said Jesus unto his disciples, If any man will come after me, let him deny himself, and take up his cross, and follow me" (Matthew 16:24).

Like a rock star or a famous athlete, Jesus often had to deal with crowd control (Luke 8:45; 12:1; Mark 3:9; 5:24). People wanted to see Him, be near Him, touch Him. In Luke 5:1 the word "pressed" suggests that they were stretching to reach Him. People have often been seriously injured, even killed, by crowds trying to get to someone.

Crowds gathered to hear Jesus because He spoke as no man had ever spoken (John 7:46) and He did things that no one had ever done (Matthew 15:30; John 3:2). The "common people heard Him gladly" (Mark 12:37). We might think that after fishing all night (Luke 5:5) the disciples would have gone home instead of listening to another sermon; but they stayed, for they, too, loved to hear Jesus preach.

What lessons do we learn from Luke 5:1–11?

Make Jesus your favorite preacher

Of all those we might pick as our hero, Jesus is the best. Everything about Jesus Christ is remarkable. Isaiah said His name would be called "Wonderful" (Isaiah 9:6)—and He is wonderful! Angels sang at His birth (Luke 2:13–14), God spoke at His baptism (Mark 1:9–11), and the sun refused to shine at His death (Matthew 27:45). Of Him, His condemner judged, "I find no fault in him" (Luke 23:4), His fellow sufferer said, He "hath done nothing amiss" (Luke 23:41), and His executioner admitted, "Certainly this was a righteous man" (Luke 23:47).

Jesus is the world's preeminent teacher (John 3:2). No teacher or personality has ever inspired others the way Jesus has. Socrates taught for forty years, Plato for fifty, and Aristotle for forty. Jesus taught for only three-and-a-half years. Yet Christ's influence far surpasses the impact left by the great philosophers' one hundred thirty years of teaching. On one occasion, the Pharisees stirred up the chief priests to send officers to arrest Him. The officers came back without Him. When asked why, they said, "Never man spake like this man" (John 7:45–46). They failed to arrest Him—disobeyed their superiors—simply because they found His sermon so interesting! When He spoke, people listened, "for he taught them as one having authority, and not as the scribes" (Matthew 7:29). His teaching is perfect, and never needs updating (John 1:17; 8:32; cf. 14:15; Hebrews 13:8).

The profound teachings of this humble Galilean carpenter lift Jesus into a category by Himself. Consider His standard of "Love your enemies" (Matthew 5:44), or "Pray for them which despitefully use you," or "Give, and it shall be given to you" (Luke 6:38). Almost all historians, even unbelievers, agree that the world would be a better place if everyone followed His teachings. Spend your lifetime studying Jesus and learning as much as you can about Him. Make Him your favorite preacher.

Launch out into the deep for Jesus

When Jesus finished His sermon, He said, "Launch out into the deep, and let down your nets for a draught" (Luke 5:4). In our language He said, "I'm through teaching. Let's go fishing! Take the boat to the deep water for a good catch of fish." Peter helped Jesus preach; Jesus will help him fish.

God wants us to launch out into the deep, that is, try great things for Him. Fishermen in Jesus' day normally fished in shallow water. Just as Jesus wanted them to go deeper, we need to launch out into deeper Christianity. Some have just enough religion to make them unhappy. They are conscious of Christ's restrictions, but not His rewards; His yoke, but not His power. We must let go of the world completely before Christ will make us happy (Luke 9:62; James 4:4; 1 Peter 2:11; 1 John 2:15–17).

We cannot be like someone learning to swim while keeping one toe on the ground. We will never enjoy swimming until all four limbs get involved! It works only by committing ourselves completely to the water. We can never enjoy Christianity until we completely leave the bottom—the world—and fully commit ourselves to Christ (Luke 14:26).

Jesus was a big thinker. He talked of taking the gospel to all nations; yea, the whole world (Matthew 28:19; Mark 16:15). Some would have thought it was too much to just teach all of Jerusalem, or to teach only those of the Roman Empire. But He wanted them to lift up their eyes and see the possibilities (Matthew 9:37–38).

Why dabble in life's shoals when we are called to the great sea of humanity? "Ships in harbor are safe," wrote John Shedd, "but that's not what ships are built for." We are not built to stay in safe harbors, either. To do great things with our lives, we must take some prudent risks, have some daring, take some chances for Christ. Theodore Roosevelt praised the man who "if he fails, at least fails while daring greatly." Are you ready to launch out in the deep for Jesus?

Launch out into the depths of thought. Few Christian teens read any Christian books that really tax their faculties. Since we are what we think (Proverbs 23:7), and our thinking is greatly affected by what we read, then we should read good materials. The Bible should be our first and favorite book (2 Timothy 3:14–17). Do you read the Bible every day? Many New Testament books can be read in less than fifteen minutes. The longest of them (Luke) takes less time to read than it takes to watch a movie. You can read almost any Bible chapter in less than ten minutes. Start a habit now, today, of never going to sleep unless you have read at least one chapter of God's Word that day. Paul said we are to give attention to reading (1 Timothy 4:13), and John said we would be blessed by reading (Revelation 1:3).

Don't be content, though, just to pass your eyes over a page of the Bible to check off an entry on a Bible-reading chart. Try to understand each verse and make sense of the flow of thought in each chapter. Don't be a skater; be a navigator. A skater skims over a frozen pond; a navigator launches onto an ocean with a destination in mind and crosses whatever is necessary to get there. We are to study (2 Timothy 2:15), which means "to give diligence," and to meditate upon God's Word (Psalm 1:2; 119:148; 1 Timothy 4:15).

Launch out into the depths of friendship (Proverbs 6:3; 17:17; 18:24; 27:6, 9, 10, 17). When you are with your friends, what do you talk about? Girls, boys, ballgames, malls, movies, magazines, tests? That's fine, but do you ever get below the surface? You need to learn how your close friends think; what their interests are; how you can help them become better people; and, especially, how you can strengthen their hands in God (1 Samuel 23:16). Every bubbling brook has deep pools; every friendship can have depths of thought and confidence, no matter how happy-go-lucky our personalities are.

Launch out into the depths of religion. James Francis Burns, Secretary of State under Franklin Roosevelt, once said, "I discovered at an early age that most of the difference between average people and great people can be explained in three words—and then some." Top people do what is expected of them—and then some. They are considerate of others—and then some. They meet their obligations—and then some. They are good friends—and then some. They can be counted on in an emergency—and then some. Christianity is the and-then-some religion. Jesus taught, "And whosoever shall compel thee to go a mile, go with him twain" (Matthew 5:41). Launch out into the deep with a second-mile religion.

Ask yourself, "Is my religion too shallow?" It is when Sunday services become just an exercise in staying awake and going through the motions of singing and praying. The church suffers from amateur Christians—half-consecrated, half-doubtful, half-trying (James 1:6; Revelation 3:15).

There are two ways to approach religion. We can do the irreducible minimum and not a bit more—and hate it—or we can do it to the best of our abilities with a smile on our faces. We can serve Jesus, not simply because we have to, but because we want to.

Some teens view Christianity as a "check-list" religion. Their attitude is, "How many services do I have to attend?" . . . "Do I have to come to Bible school?" . . . "Do I have to give anything? After all, I'm only a teenager." They want to do the least they can get away with—and no more. The youth who pleases God constantly asks, "What more can I do?" If we leave for a long trip, do we put just enough gas in the car to get there? No, we fill up the tank so we'll be sure to have enough to get there.

We are making a trip from earth to heaven; are we trying to put just enough oil in our lamps to make it? (Matthew 25:1–13). The historian of Alexander the Great summed up his hero in a striking phrase: "Even if he had conquered the whole of India, still he would have been reaching out beyond into the unknown." The good Samaritan's religion went the second mile (Luke 10:33–35). He helped the injured man, let him ride on his beast, paid for him to stay in an inn, and even volunteered to pay whatever else was owed.

Have you taken any chances for Christ? Have you even let others know that you are a Christian? Have you invited them to come with you to VBS or to Bible class? Make some big plans of the things you want to do for Jesus with your life.

The University of Florida football team was running sprints some years ago. Jack Katz, who played tackle, was the fastest lineman. Katz approached Coach Ray Graves to ask if he could run with the backs. For the next several days Katz finished last in every race with the backfield runners. Nobody was surprised. Coach Graves asked Katz if he wouldn't rather be a winner with the linemen than a loser with the backs. He responded, "I'm not here to outrun linemen. I already know I can do that. I'm here to learn how to run faster; and if you've noticed, I'm losing by a little less every day." God wants us to want to get better, too. Paul said we should "grow up into him in all things" (Ephesians 4:15).

Don't ever doubt what Jesus says (Luke 5:5).
Jesus' invitation to go fishing did not meet a happy reception. Peter said, "Master, we have toiled all the night, and have taken nothing," which means, "I'm sick of fishing. I just got back from fishing. I've been up all night, and it's a waste of time to go back."

Jesus was testing Peter's faith. Peter was a professional fisherman. Jesus was not a fisherman; He was a carpenter and a teacher. Did Jesus even know what He was talking about? Jesus had invaded Peter's home turf. When Jesus healed his mother-in-law (Mark 1:30–31), Peter was impressed. After all, maybe Jesus knew more about healing than Peter knew. Peter was not a doctor. But Peter knew how and where and when to catch fish. In Peter's way of thinking, if he had worked all night and caught nothing, then nobody could catch any.

We also are sometimes tempted to think we know more than Jesus. We may confine Jesus' wisdom to one day (Sunday) and one place (the church building). If the Bible teacher acts like the Bible should rule our lives at school on Monday or with our friends on Saturday night, he has gone too far. "Religion's fine in its place," we think. We listen to the lesson and think—although we may never say it—"This is for somebody else, somewhere else, but not for me, not now." If the preacher preaches on "church stuff," that's okay, but if he talks about cheating on term papers or attending church services or dancing or immodest clothing, then we tune him out. "Turn the other cheek" (Matthew 5:39) may work for the preacher; he does not function in the dog-eat-dog teen-world. "Keep thyself pure" (1 Timothy 5:22) is good for elders and old ladies at church, but not for sixteen-year-olds, we may think.

Jesus doesn't settle for confinement to the "religious compartment" of our lives. It is either first place or no place with Him. God hates to come in second. He said, "No man can serve two masters: for either he will hate the one, and love the other; or else he will hold to the one, and despise the other. Ye cannot serve God and mammon" (Matthew 6:24). To please Him, we must love Him with all our heart, mind, soul, and strength (Mark 12:29–30). God means for us to take His Word personally. Let us not doubt that

God knows what is best for our lives. He made us; He loves us; He wants us to be happy in this life and saved in the next. If the Bible says something, then let's believe and follow it.

Obey Jesus, even when it doesn't make complete sense.
Peter's objection to Jesus' command was well founded from a human viewpoint. The daytime—especially the hot part of the day—was not good for fishing. In addition, they were tired and had just cleaned their nets. It just did not make sense to go fishing right then. Still, Peter reluctantly obeyed. By using the word "nevertheless" (Luke 5:5), he showed he was obeying under protest. Later, he saw that Jesus knew what He was talking about and repented of this hesitant faith.

When the Lord Christ gives a command, we need not argue and say, "We've tried it and it won't work." The Duke of Wellington once gave a command to a general, who answered that it was impossible to do. Wellington told him, "You go ahead and do it, because I don't give impossible commands." Jesus does not give impossible commands, either. John said "his commandments are not grievous" (1 John 5:3). As Christ's servants (John 15:14; Romans 1:1; 16:1; Colossians 4:12; 2 Timothy 2:24; James 1:1; 2 Peter 1:1; Revelation 1:1), we do not question orders. A strong faith in God will cause us to attempt what seems hopeless. Jesus once asked, "And why call ye me, Lord, Lord, and do not the things which I say?" (Luke 6:46). Good servants obey, regardless.

Success comes at the point of obedience. Without it, great blessings are forfeited. Naaman almost went home to die a leper, because God's way made no sense to him. He was saved when a servant talked him into obeying God (2 Kings 5:10–14). Many people go to Judgment unprepared because baptism did not make sense to them (1 Peter 3:21). It is our task to get them to see that success comes at the point of trusting Jesus enough to do what He says. Trust and obey, for there is no other way.

Peter committed himself to a course he knew would make him look ridiculous in the eyes of other fishermen. To cast nets under these circumstances would not make sense to anyone who saw him do it. Still, he did it.

He cared more about what Jesus thought than what others thought. Even when obeying God's commands makes us look foolish, we should humbly submit to them (Galatians 1:10). At the wedding feast at Cana, Mary gave the servants good advice: "Whatsoever he saith unto you, do it" (John 2:5). Our friends may make fun of us if we refuse to dress the way they dress (1 Timothy 2:9–10), drink what they drink (Proverbs 20:1), laugh at what they find humorous (Ephesians 5:12), and go where they go (1 Peter 4:4). But what Christ thinks of us is more important than what they think of us.

Some scorned Jesus, too. He warned us: "But when they persecute you in this city, flee ye into another . . . The disciple is not above his master, nor the servant above his lord. It is enough for the disciple that he be as his master, and the servant as his lord. If they have called the master of the house Beelzebub, how much more shall they call them of his household?" (Matthew 10:23–25).

Acknowledge your unworthiness to be with Jesus

"When Simon Peter saw it, he fell down at Jesus' knees, saying, Depart from me; for I am a sinful man, O Lord" (Luke 5:8). Peter's conscience had been asleep, but this miracle startled it awake. He needed, as we do, both complacency and conceit taken out of him. Peter felt the penetrating gaze that had detected the fish, reading his heart's deepest secrets.

Donald Godwin took his four-year-old grandson camping at Lake Superior. When a bad thunderstorm came up, the little guy was fascinated by the flashes of "whitening." He watched the sky light up for several minutes and then gave his commentary: "Look! Jesus is taking my picture." Our activities and attitudes never escape God's attention. It is as if God is constantly taking our picture.

Peter now saw himself as a beggar looking for a handout from God (Matthew 5:3). We may try to excuse our sins, but sin is no small thing. One songwriter aptly stated our case:

> *Nothing in my hand I bring;*
> *Simply to Thy cross I cling;*

Naked, come to Thee for dress;
Helpless, look to Thee for grace.
Foul, I to the fountain fly.
Wash me, Savior, or I die.

We expect Peter to say, "Lord, I tremble before one who can do such things." Why does he say: "Depart from me, I am a sinner"? In the context, Peter is confessing the sin of earlier reluctant obedience. This teaches that obedience is unacceptable if accompanied by complaining. We should follow the Savior with joy (Philippians 4:4), and without any reservations or grumbling complaints. It is a privilege to be a child of God!

Let Jesus astonish you

Imagine Peter's feelings when his hand felt the net tighten! Where there had been no fish the night before, there now are hundreds. Jesus' miraculous knowledge enabled Him to find fish under water as easily as we find birds in the air (cf. John 21:6). All things—particularly the fish of the sea and "whatsoever passeth through the paths of the sea" (Psalm 8:8)—had been put under Jesus' feet.

Peter and his partners caught so many fish that the net broke and they almost sank two boats in getting them to shore! To overload two five-ton boats—the likely size—meant this was a vast quantity of fish. Peter and the others were astonished.

Peter caught a glimpse of God's power in Jesus. He had seen Jesus for who He was: the holy one of God. Here in a small boat in a small corner of the world was God's Son Himself. What does one do in God's presence? Peter fell down in humility, reverence, and awe. When we see God's power in nature (Psalm 19:1–6) and in His Word (Psalm 19:7–13), we bow before Him, too. As sinners, we should also throw ourselves at Jesus' feet as we are confronted with the Bible's record of His miracles, power, love, and sacrifice for us.

Our worship services are for praising God (Psalm 29:1–2; 66:1–2; 71:8, 14; 92:1–8; 95:1–7; 150:6; Acts 2:47; Jude 1:25; Revelation 7:12). We praise by singing (Ephesians 5:19; Colossians 3:16; cf. Exodus 15:1; 32:18), praying, and studying His Word. Church services are not for visiting friends, being entertained, finding a girlfriend or boyfriend, seeing and be seen, or fulfilling a duty. They are not even primarily a time to learn the Bible or gain spiritual strength, although these are good by-products. If we do not praise God in our services, then we have wasted our time (1 Peter 5:11).

The Hebrew word for *praise* (*halal*) means, "to shout." From it we get *hallelujah*—"praise Jehovah." This does not mean we should shout out in our services, for everything must be done "decently and in order" (1 Corinthians 14:40). But it does show the energy we should use in worshipping God. At Jesus' birth, angels praised saying, "Glory to God in the highest" (Luke 2:13–14). If we had the tongues of angels and the voice of birds, we could not praise God as He deserves (cf. Revelation 5:13). If we were born speaking praises and had breath so we need never cease, we could not adequately praise His name. If every rock could speak, it would praise God (Luke 19:37–40). If the stars could sing, their song would be one of praise.

Launch out with Jesus. It will be the voyage of a lifetime.

Discussion Questions

1. What kind of preacher do you think Jesus was? Why do you think it would have been like to hear Him?

2. Why is Jesus the best hero a teen can have?

3. Why did those who came to arrest Jesus on one occasion return to their superiors without Him?

4. What are some of the teachings of Jesus that set Him apart from any other teacher of ancient times?

5. Explain what it means to "launch out into the deep with Jesus."

6. How can teens launch out into the deep in these areas (pick your favorite from this list and discuss):

a. Thought?
   b. Religion?
   c. Friendship?

7. Is Christianity meant to be a "checklist religion"?

8. Name some ways that teens seem to think that they know more than Jesus knows.

9. Does Jesus give impossible commands?

10. How does Peter's response, "Depart from me; for I am a sinful man" show an attitude that teens should possess?

11. What astonishes you most about Jesus?

12. For us to get more out of worship, what likely needs to happen? Discuss your answer.
    a. The worship needs to change (externals).
    b. The worshipper needs to change (internals).

ENDNOTES

Chapter 5

1. http://www.4women.gov/quitsmoking/fastfacts.cfm.
2. http://www.teendrugabuse.us/teensmoking.html.
3. Seven percent of kids in ninth grade reported smoking cigarettes. The rate of smoking then increases to a high of 26 percent in twelfth grade.
4. The American Medical Women's Association has 3,000 (http://www.amwa-doc.org/).
5. A report published in the *American Journal of Preventive Medicine* (Vol. 27, No. 4: 267–276), revealed that about half of the students said they bought cigarettes themselves from some type of retail store, often convenience stores or gas stations. Few students had to provide proof of age, even though all fifty states and the District of Columbia restrict tobacco sales to minors. "It doesn't take many who are breaking the rules to provide an outlet to a lot of kids," Johnston said. "Word gets around where you can get away with buying cigarettes, either because you can use a false ID, or they don't check, or they don't care." Just 25 percent of eighth graders, 36 percent of tenth graders, and 40 percent of twelfth graders reported having to show ID to make their purchase.
6. http://usgovinfo.about.com/od/healthcare/a/kidsgetsmokes.htm.
7. http://www.youngwomenshealth.org/smokeinfo.html.
8. http://en.wikipedia.org/wiki/Tobacco_smoking#Link_between_tobacco_use_and_use_of_illicit_drugs.
9. http://www.whyquit.com/whyquit/LinksAAddiction.html.
10. http://www.youngwomenshealth.org/smokeinfo.html.
11. http://www.youngwomenshealth.org/smokeinfo.html.
12. http://www.specialolympics.org/Special+Olympics+Public+Website/ English/Coach/Coaching_Guides/ Nutrition+Safety+and+Fitness/Things+to+Keep+Athletes+Tobacco-Free.htm.
13. http://www2.mdanderson.org/depts/oncolog/articles/05/6-jun/6-05-1.html.
14. http://www.athleteproject.com/member/sportspharm.htm.
15. http://moneycentral.msn.com/content/Insurance/Insureyourhealth/P100291.asp.
16. To state this more correctly, they refuse to hire those who "create a hazardous work environment, not for smoking."
17. http://medicolegal.tripod.com/donthire.htm.
18. http://www.parapundit.com/archives/002602.html.
19. http://www.msnbc.msn.com/id/10296844/.
20. http://articles.moneycentral.msn.com/Insurance/InsureYourHealth/HighCostOfSmoking.aspx?page=1.
21. http://www.parapundit.com/archives/002602.html.
22. After announcing it would no longer employ smokers, Weyco fired four employees who refused to submit to a breath test (http://moneycentral.msn.com).
23. http://www.medicalnewstoday.com/medicalnews.php?newsid=66527.
24. In 2004, the average American worked 1,777 hours a year, which broken down 8/day, is 222 days a year. ftp://ftp.bls.gov/pub/special.requests/opt/lpr/histmfgsic.zip.
25. http://moneycentral.msn.com/content/Insurance/Insureyourhealth/P100291.asp.
26. http://medicolegal.tripod.com/donthire.htm.

Chapter 6

1. The average retail price of a pack of cigarettes in the United States is $4.11, plus sales tax (http://www.cdc.gov/tobacco/data_statistics/Factsheets/economic_facts.htm).
2. This is a conservative estimate. Another source has 18 cigarettes per day for Americans, 15 per day world average (http://library.thinkquest.org/17360/tb-e-stt.html). Further, men who started smoking before the age of 15 smoked on average 5.5 cigarettes more than those who started at age 19 or over. Women who started smoking early in life smoked, on average, 6.8 cigarettes/day more than women who started later. http://www.ncbi.nlm.nih.gov/entrez/query.fcgi?cmd=Retrieve&db=PubMed&list_uids=10090865&dopt=Abstract.
3. Addicted smokers tend to use more nicotine over time. The habit usually grows. What starts out as 5 or 10 cigarettes a day usually becomes a pack or two a day habit.
4. Ninety percent of smokers start smoking before age 18 (http://www2.mdanderson.org/depts/oncolog/articles/05/6-jun/6-05-1.html).

ENDNOTES

5   Smokers pay about $33 of the cost, their families absorb about $7, and others pay a little less than $1.50. Incidental costs such as higher cleaning bills and lower resale values on smoky cars were not included.
6   http://www.dukemagazine.duke.edu/dukemag/issues/030405/depgaz12.html.
7   http://moneycentral.msn.com/content/Insurance/Insureyourhealth/P100291.asp.
8   http://findarticles.com/p/articles/mi_m0826/is_n5_v9/ai_14244371.
9   http://healthliteracy.worlded.org/docs/tobacco/Unit3/1why_people_ smoke.html.
10 In a study of nearly 12,000 pre- and postmenopausal women aged 40 to 73, the WHR increased as the number of cigarettes smoked per day increased (http://www.ash.org.uk/html/factsheets/html/fact10.html).
11 http://www.teenboardingschools.com/teensmoking.htm.
12 Jack E. Henningfield, PhD, is Adjunct Professor of Behavioral Biology, Department of Psychiatry and Behavioral Sciences at the Johns Hopkins University School of Medicine, and Vice President for Research and Health Policy at Pinney Associates. Dr. Henningfield was selected to be the new Director of The Robert Wood Johnson Foundation's Innovators Combating Substance Abuse Awards Program at the Johns Hopkins University School of Medicine in December 2002.
13 http://www.lycaeum.org/drugwar/hening.html.
14 http://www.teenboardingschools.com/teensmoking.htm.
15 http://www.youngwomenshealth.org/smokeinfo.html.
16 http://www.4women.gov/quitsmoking/fastfacts.cfm.

Chapter 11
1   http://www.mediarelations.k-state.edu/WEB/News/Webzine/Didyouhearyes/.
2   daterapefacts.html.
3   http://www.mediarelations.k-state.edu/WEB/News/Webzine/Didyouhearyes/.
4   daterapefacts.html.
5   http://www.mediarelations.k-state.edu/WEB/News/Webzine/Didyouhearyes/.
6   http://www2.truman.edu/~aweitz/prevent_date_rape/prevention_recommendations.php.
7   Abbey, A.; Ross, L. T.; McDuffie, D.; McAuslan, P. Alcohol and dating risk factors for sexual assault among college women. *Psychology of Women Quarterly* 1996; 20(1), 147–169.
8   http://www.mediarelations.k-state.edu/WEB/News/Webzine/Didyouhearyes/daterapefacts.html.
9   http://www.ehow.com/tips_8557.html.
10 E. Tenn. School of Preaching, "Living Soberly, Righteously, and Godly" David Fickling, Monday November 21, 2005.
11 http://www.womenagainstrape.net/PressCoverage/Oneinthree.htm.
12 David Fickling, Monday November 21, 2005, http://www.womenagainstrape.net/PressCoverage/Oneinthree.htm.
13 http://www2.truman.edu/~aweitz/prevent_date_rape/research_findings_negative_expectation.htm.
14 http://en.wikipedia.org/wiki/Date_rape.
15 http://www.mediarelations.k-state.edu/WEB/News/Webzine/Didyouhearyes/daterapefacts.html.
16 http://www.police.ufl.edu/csd/csd_safetytips_daterape.asp.
17 Abbey, A.; Ross, L. T.; Mcduffie, D.; Mcauslan, P. Alcohol and dating risk factors for sexual assault among college women. *Psychology of Women Quarterly* 1996; 20(1), 147–169.
18 http://www.police.ufl.edu/csd/csd_safetytips_daterape.asp,

Chapter 12
1   http://en.wikipedia.org/wiki/Date_rape.
2   http://www.mediarelations.k-state.edu/WEB/News/Webzine/Didyouhearyes/daterapefacts.html.
3   David Fickling, Monday November 21, 2005, http://www. womenagainstrape.net/ PressCoverage/Oneinthree.htm.
4   This phrase means to make "stronger and more inebriating by the addition of more powerful ingredients, as honey, spices, myrrh, defrutum, opiates" (*Treasury of Scripture Knowledge*).
5   Old word from *asōtos,* in New Testament only three times (here, Titus 1:6; 1 Peter 4:4) (adverb *asō̄tō̄s* in Luke 15:13).
6   http://www.higheredcenter.org/pubs/rapefly.htm.
7   http://www.higheredcenter.org/pubs/rapefly.htm.

Chapter 13
1. All other statistics quoted in this article (unless otherwise noted), are from "Where True Love Waits," Cathi Woods, *Christianity Today*.
2. Number of new hepatitis B cases : 6212 (2004). / Number of new tuberculosis cases: 14,517 (2004). Number of new syphilis cases: 33,401 (2004). / Number of new chlamydia cases: 929,462 (2004). Number of new gonorrhea cases: 330,132 (2004). / Number of new salmonella cases: 42,197 (2004). Number of new Acquired Immunodeficiency Syndrome (AIDS) cases: 42,514 (2004). Health, United States: 2006, tables 51–52.

Chapter 14
1. *phthora*, "decay, i.e. ruin (spontaneous or inflicted)."
2. Much of this research is found at the Web site for Proven Men Ministries, Ltd., 16011 Chieftain Ave., Rockville, MD, 20855 (http://www.1wayout.org/pages/need.aspx). No endorsement of all content is implied, but one may find much additional useful information at this site.
3. According to the U.S. Census Population clock, which takes birth/death rates and census figures and updates into account, at 11:19 EST March 23, 2004, there were 292,859,499 Americans.
4. Results of MSNBC.com, the number one Internet news site, 2000 Online Cybersex Survey, printed by Business Wire, July 19, 2001. The MSNBC online poll is believed to be the largest Internet study of online sexuality to date. The survey received responses from over 38,000 users. MSNBC Web site surveys are self-selected and unscientific, not the random samples utilized by polling organizations. In 1999, the National Council on Sexual Addiction Compulsivity estimated that 6 to 8 percent of Americans are sex addicts. (Cooper, Alvin, Dana E. Putnam, Lynn A. Planchon, and Sylvain C. Boies "Online Sexual Compulsivity: Getting Tangled in the Net," Sexual Addiction and Compulsivity, 6:79–104. Taken from Amparano, J. "Sex addicts get help." *The Arizona Republic*, p. A1, 1999). Even with a much more narrowly defined definition, the range of those sexually addicted remains between 3 to 6 percent. Jennifer P. Schneider, M.D., PhD; National Council on Sexual Addiction and Compulsivity Web site, October 2000.
5. Sexual Addiction and Compulsivity: The Journal of Treatment and Prevention, Spring, 2000. Based on 1998 survey of 9265 adults by Dr. Alvin Cooper and others.
6. The Parsonage®, Battle Plan Against Pornography, Sermon Outline, printed at Family.org.
7. Linz, D., Donnerstein, E., & Adams, S. M. (1989), 509–522.
8. "Vile Passions," an article on the effect of pornography reprinted in the AFA Journal, August 2002, by Rusty Benson.
9. "Legitimate Violence, Violent Attitudes, and Rape: A State-Level Analysis" (with Larry Baron and Murray A. Straus). Annals of the New York Academy of Sciences, Vol. 528, 1988.
10. O'Brien, Shirley. 1992. Child Pornography (Dubuque: Kendall/Hunt Publishing Company).
11. The Parsonage®, citing Dr. Gene Abel, Emory University.
12. "Sexuality, Contraception, and the Media," American Academy of Pediatrics Committee on Public Education, Pediatrics, Vol. 107 No. 1, Policy Statement (January 2001, pp. 191–194) (January 2001).
13. The Parsonage®.
14. Holmes and De Burger (1988).

Chapter 15
1. Robyn Gearey, "The Numbers Game," The New Republic, May 19, 1997, p. 20.
2. Paul Tharp, "Lottery Raises Issues of Cents and Sensibilities," New York Post, November 14, 1997.
3. http://mdickson.com/blog/uncategorized/4/.
4. Cox.
5. http://media.www.iowastatedaily.com/media/storage/paper818/news/ 2003/07/24/Opinion/Column.Winning.The.Lottery.May.Not.Be.A.Dream.Come.True-1096029.shtml.
6. http://www.savingadvice.com/forums/other/5559-probability-winning-lottery-dont-waste-your-money.html.
7. http://www.pittsburghlive.com/x/pittsburghtrib/s_385745.html. Sources: "Life: The Odds," by Gregory Baer; National Center for Health Statistics, CDC; American Lung Association; American Cancer Society; National Safety Council; International Federation of Red Cross and Red Crescent Societies; World Health Organization; USGS; Clark Chapman, SwRI; David Morrison, NASA; Michael Paine, Planetary Society Australian Volunteers.